Learn French For Kids

Learn The Most Commonly Used French Grammar Like Crazy With Fun and Exciting Language Lessons for Children. Take Your Child From Beginner To Intermediate By Taking The Lesson on The Go, In The Car, or During Travel.

Aimon Caron

Table of Contents

Introduction

Using a foreign language is a must in our current societies, as we live in a global society in which you will have to talk to people who don't speak English and you may need to use this foreign language. It will be useful in your everyday life, if you want to talk to foreigners, know more about this other culture and use it at work.

This book will help you learn French quickly and easily with a specific method. There is no cultural explanation about the meaning of each word and no detailed grammar rule, but only a list of words, their spelling and their use in a specific situation. It is composed of a series of themes or chapter with the words you need to know and dialogs. That means you can use it for each situation you need. You are at school and you need to use greetings in French: go to the dedicated chapter and you will know which words to use and how to use them in a sentence.

The method is also easy for you to learn French quickly: you have first a list of words to know, then short dialogs which are common examples and practices.

Learning French requires specific lessons such as those you get at school, but you also need to learn by yourself and this book is a useful tool to help you learn French.

Learning French is possible and easy with us! Let's begin now!

CHAPTER 1: THE BASICS

Whether at home or at school, you use colours and figures every day to describe an object or to express the time. It's the same in French, you will need the basics in your everyday conversations. You also need to use figures and numbers to quantify -to count- objects or to mention the date. Let's get started.

COLOURS

Vocabulary

English word Word	French
White	**blanc**
Underbleached	**écru**
Beige	**beige**
Yellow	**jaune**
Ochre	**ocre**
Orange	**orange**
Pink	**rose**
Red	**rouge**
Burgundy	**bordeaux**

English word Word	French
Brown	**marron**
Hazel	**noisette**
Grey	**gris**
Dark	**noir**
Blue	**bleu**
Light-blue	**bleu-ciel**

| Navy-blue | **bleu-marine** | Emerald | **émeraude** |
| Green | **vert** | | |

Dialogs

Dialog 1

What colour is your bike? **Quelle est la couleur de ton vélo ?**

My bike is blue. **Mon vélo est bleu.**

Dialog 2

Do you like black cats? **Aimes-tu les chats noirs ?**

Of course, I do. **Bien sûr, j'aime bien.**

Dialog 3

What colour are your eyes? **Quelle est la couleur de tes yeux ?**

I have got green eyes. **J'ai les yeux verts.**

Dialog 4

What is your favourite colour? **Quelle est ta couleur préférée ?**

My favourite colour is yellow. **Ma couleur préférée est le jaune.**

Practice

English :   blue

French :   **bleu**

Repeat :   **bleu**

Repeat :   **bleu**

Spell :   **b-l-e-u**

Spell :   **b-l-e-u**

In a phrase : **Mon vélo est bleu.** *My bike is blue.*

Repeat :   **Mon vélo est bleu.** *My bike is blue.*

Repeat :   **Mon vélo est bleu.** *My bike is blue.*

Repeat :   **Mon vélo est bleu.** *My bike is blue.*

English :   black

French :   **noir**

Repeat :   **noir**

Repeat :   **noir**

Spell :   **n-o-i-r**

Spell :   **n-o-i-r**

In a phrase : **Aimes-tu les chats noirs ?** *Do you like black cats?*

Repeat : **Aimes-tu les chats noirs ?** *Do you like black cats?*

Repeat : **Aimes-tu les chats noirs ?** *Do you like black cats?*

Repeat : **Aimes-tu les chats noirs ?** *Do you like black cats?*

English : green

French : **vert**

Repeat : **vert**

Repeat : **vert**

Spell : **v-e-r-t**

Spell : **v-e-r-t**

In a phrase : **J'ai les yeux verts.** *I have got green eyes.*

Repeat : **J'ai les yeux verts.** *I have got green eyes.*

Repeat : **J'ai les yeux verts.** *I have got green eyes.*

Repeat : **J'ai les yeux verts.** *I have got green eyes.*

English :   yellow

French :   **jaune**

Repeat :   **jaune**

Repeat :   **jaune**

Spell :   **j-a-u-n-e**

Spell :   **j-a-u-n-e**

In a phrase :   **Ma couleur préférée est le jaune.** *My favourite colour is yellow.*

Repeat :   **Ma couleur préférée est le jaune.** *My favourite colour is yellow.*

Repeat :   **Ma couleur préférée est le jaune.** *My favourite colour is yellow.*

Repeat :   **Ma couleur préférée est le jaune.** *My favourite colour is yellow.*

NUMBERS

Vocabulary

English word	French		
word			
One	**un**	Two	**deux**
		Three	**trois**
		Four	**quatre**

Five	cinq
Six	six
Seven	sept
Eight	huit
Nine	neuf
Ten	dix

English word word	French
Eleven	onze
Twelve	douze
Thirteen	treize
Fourteen	quatorze
Fifteen	quinze
Sixteen	seize
Seventeen	dix-sept
Eighteen	dix-huit
Nineteen	dix-neuf

| Twenty | vingt |

English word word	French
Twenty-one	vingt-et-un
Twenty-two	vingt-deux
Thirty	trente
Thirty-one	trente-et-un
Forty	quarante
Fifty	cinquante
Sixty	soixante
Seventy	soixante-dix
Eighty	quatre-vingt

English word word	French

Ninety	**quatre-vingt-dix**	One thousand	**mille**
One hundred	**cent**	Ten thousand	**dix milles**
One hundred-and-one	**cent-un**	One million	**un million**
One hundred-and-ten	**cent-dix**	One billion	**un milliard**
Two hundred	**deux-cents**		

Dialogs

<u>Dialog 1</u>

| How many brothers do you have? | **Combien de frères as-tu ?** |
| I have two brothers. | **J'ai deux frères.** |

<u>Dialog 2</u>

| How old are you? | **Quel âge as-tu ?** |
| I am eleven years old. | **J'ai onze ans.** |

<u>Dialog 3</u>

| How many books do you have? | **Combien de livres as-tu ?** |
| I have four books. | **J'ai quatre livres.** |

<u>Dialog 4</u>

Which mark did you get at school? **Quelle note as-tu obtenu à l'école ?**

I got an A (eighteen out of twenty). **J'ai eu un A (dix-huit sur vingt).**

Practice

English :   two

French :   **deux**

Repeat :   **deux**

Repeat :   **deux**

Spell :   **d-e-u-x**

Spell :   **d-e-u-x**

In a phrase : **J'ai deux frères.** *I have two brothers.*

Repeat :   **J'ai deux frères.** *I have two brothers.*

Repeat :   **J'ai deux frères.** *I have two brothers.*

Repeat :   **J'ai deux frères.** *I have two brothers.*

English :   eleven

French :   **onze**

Repeat :   **onze**

Repeat :   **onze**

Spell :   **o-n-z-e**

Spell :   **o-n-z-e**

In a phrase :   **J'ai onze ans.**   *I am eleven years old.*

Repeat :   **J'ai onze ans.**   *I am eleven years old.*

Repeat :   **J'ai onze ans.**   *I am eleven years old.*

Repeat :   **J'ai onze ans.**   *I am eleven years old.*

English :   four

French :   **quatre**

Repeat :   **quatre**

Repeat :   **quatre**

Spell :   **q-u-a-t-r-e**

Spell :   **q-u-a-t-r-e**

In a phrase :   **J'ai quatre livres.**   *I have four books.*

Repeat :   **J'ai quatre livres.**   *I have four books.*

Repeat :   **J'ai quatre livres.**   *I have four books.*

Repeat :   **J'ai quatre livres.**   *I have four books.*

English :   eighteen

French :   **dix-huit**

Repeat :   **dix-huit**

Repeat :   **dix-huit**

Spell :   **d-i-x-h-u-i-t**

Spell :   **d-i-x-h-u-i-t**

In a phrase :   **J'ai eu un A (dix-huit sur vingt).**   *I got an A (eighteen out of twenty).*

Repeat :   **J'ai eu un A (dix-huit sur vingt).**   *I got an A (eighteen out of twenty).*

Repeat :   **J'ai eu un A (dix-huit sur vingt).**   *I got an A (eighteen out of twenty).*

Repeat :   **J'ai eu un A (dix-huit sur vingt).**   *I got an A (eighteen out of twenty).*

ORDINAL NUMBERS

Vocabulary

<u>English word</u>   <u>French</u>   The first   **le**
<u>word</u>   **premier**

English word	French word
The second	le **deuxième**
The third	le **troisième**
The fourth	le **quatrième**
The fifth	le **cinquième**
The sixth	le **sixième**
The seventh	le **septième**
The eighth	le **huitième**
The ninth	le **neuvième**
The tenth	le **dixième**
The eleventh	le **onzième**
The twelfth	le **douzième**
The thirteenth	le **treizième**

English word	French word
The fourteenth	**le quatorzième**
The fifteenth	le **quinzième**
The sixteenth	le **seizième**
The seventeenth	**le dix-septième**
The eighteenth	**le dix-huitième**
The nineteenth	**le dix-neuvième**
The twentieth	**le vingtième**
The twenty-first	**le vingt-et-unième**
The twenty-second	**le vingt-deuxième**
The thirtieth	**le trentième**
The fortieth	**le quarantième**

The fiftieth **le cinquantième**

The hundredth **le centième**

The sixtieth **le soixantième**

The hundred and first **le cent-unième**

The seventieth **le soixante-dixième**

The thousandth **le millier**

The eightieth **le quatre-vingtième**

The millionth **le millionième**

The ninetieth **le quatre-ving-dixième**

The billionth **le milliardième**

Dialogs

Dialog 1

What have you read already? **Qu'as-tu déjà lu ?**

I have read the first chapter. **J'ai lu le premier chapitre.**

Dialog 2

What is your rank at the game? **Quel est ton classement au jeu ?**

I am the second. **Je suis le deuxième.**

Dialog 3

Which choice did you make? **Quel choix as-tu fait ?**

I've chosen the third option. **J'ai choisi la troisième option.**

Dialog 4

When did you go on holidays?   **Quand es-tu parti en vacances ?**

We left the fifth day of the week.   **Nous sommes partis le cinquième jour de la semaine.**

Practice

English :   first

French :   **premier**

Repeat :   **premier**

Repeat :   **premier**

Spell :   **p-r-e-m-i-e-r**

Spell :   **p-r-e-m-i-e-r**

In a phrase : **J'ai lu le premier chapitre.** *I have read the first chapter.*

Repeat :   **J'ai lu le premier chapitre.** *I have read the first chapter.*

Repeat :   **J'ai lu le premier chapitre.** *I have read the first chapter.*

Repeat :   **J'ai lu le premier chapitre.** *I have read the first chapter.*

English :   second

French :   **deuxième**

Repeat :   **deuxième**

Repeat :   **deuxième**

Spell :   **d-e-u-x-i-è-m-e**

Spell :   **d-e-u-x-i-è-m-e**

In a phrase : **Je suis le deuxième.**   *I am the second.*

Repeat :   **Je suis le deuxième.**   *I am the second.*

Repeat :   **Je suis le deuxième.**   *I am the second.*

Repeat :   **Je suis le deuxième.**   *I am the second.*

English :   third

French :   **troisième**

Repeat :   **troisième**

Repeat :   **troisième**

Spell :   **t-r-o-i-s-i-è-m-e**

Spell :   **t-r-o-i-s-i-è-m-e**

In a phrase : **J'ai choisi la troisième option.**   *I've chosen the third option.*

Repeat :   **J'ai choisi la troisième option.** *I've chosen the third option.*

Repeat :   **J'ai choisi la troisième option.** *I've chosen the third option.*

Repeat :   **J'ai choisi la troisième option.** *I've chosen the third option.*

English :   fifth

French :   **cinquième**

Repeat :   **cinquième**

Repeat :   **cinquième**

Spell :   **c-i-n-q-u-i-è-m-e**

Spell :   **c-i-n-q-u-i-è-m-e**

In a phrase : **Nous sommes partis le cinquième jour de la semaine.** *We left the fifth day of the week.*

Repeat :   **Nous sommes partis le cinquième jour de la semaine.** *We left the fifth day of the week.*

Repeat :   **Nous sommes partis le cinquième jour de la semaine.** *We left the fifth day of the week.*

Repeat :   **Nous sommes partis le cinquième jour de la semaine.** *We left the fifth day of the week.*

DAYS & MONTHS

Vocabulary

<u>English word word</u>	<u>French</u>	<u>English word word</u>	<u>French</u>
Monday	**lundi**	March	**mars**
Tuesday	**mardi**	April	**avril**
Wednesday	**mercredi**	May	**mai**
Thursday	**jeudi**	June	**juin**
Friday	**vendredi**	July	**juillet**
Saturday	**samedi**	August	**août**
Sunday	**dimanche**	September	**septembre**
January	**janvier**	October	**octobre**
February	**février**	November	**novembre**
		December	**décembre**

Dialogs

<u>Dialog 1</u>

When does the new lesson start? **Quand la nouvelle leçon commence-t-elle ?**

It will start next Monday. **Elle va commencer lundi prochain.**

<u>Dialog 2</u>

How often do you go to the swimming pool? **À quelle fréquence vas-tu à la piscine ?**

I go to the swimming pool every Wednesday. **Je vais à la piscine tous les mercredis.**

<u>Dialog 3</u>

When will you watch the movie? **Quand vas-tu regarder le film ?**

I will watch the movie on Friday evening. **Je regarderai le film vendredi soir.**

<u>Dialog 4</u>

What's the date, today? **Quel jour sommes-nous aujourd'hui ?**

Today is the first of October, 2020. **Nous sommes le premier octobre 2020.**

Practice

English :   Monday

French :   **lundi**

Repeat :   **lundi**

Repeat :   **lundi**

Spell :   **l-u-n-d-i**

Spell :   **l-u-n-d-i**

In a phrase :   **Elle va commencer lundi prochain.**   *It will start next Monday.*

Repeat :   **Elle va commencer lundi prochain.**   *It will start next Monday.*

Repeat :   **Elle va commencer lundi prochain.**   *It will start next Monday.*

Repeat :   **Elle va commencer lundi prochain.**   *It will start next Monday.*

English :   Wednesday

French :   **mercredi**

Repeat :   **mercredi**

Repeat :   **mercredi**

Spell :   **m-e-r-c-r-e-d-i**

Spell :   **m-e-r-c-r-e-d-i**

In a phrase : **Je vais à la piscine tous les mercredis.** *I go to the swimming-pool every Wednesday.*

Repeat :   **Je vais à la piscine tous les mercredis.** *I go to the swimming-pool every Wednesday.*

Repeat :   **Je vais à la piscine tous les mercredis.** *I go to the swimming-pool every Wednesday.*

Repeat :   **Je vais à la piscine tous les mercredis.** *I go to the swimming-pool every Wednesday.*

English :   Friday

French :   **vendredi**

Repeat :   **vendredi**

Repeat :   **vendredi**

Spell :   **v-e-n-d-r-e-d-i**

Spell :   **v-e-n-d-r-e-d**-i

In a phrase : **Je regarderai le film vendredi soir.**   *I will watch the movie on Friday evening.*

Repeat :   **Je regarderai le film vendredi soir.**   *I will watch the movie on Friday evening.*

Repeat :   **Je regarderai le film vendredi soir.**   *I will watch the movie on Friday evening.*

Repeat :   **Je regarderai le film vendredi soir.**   *I will watch the movie on Friday evening.*

English :   October

French :   **octobre**

Repeat :   **octobre**

Repeat :   **octobre**

Spell :   **o-c-t-o-b-e-r**

Spell :   **o-c-t-o-b-e-r**

In a phrase :   **Nous sommes le premier octobre 2020.**   *Today is the first of October, 2020.*

Repeat :   **Nous sommes le premier octobre 2020.**   *Today is the first of October, 2020.*

Repeat :   **Nous sommes le premier octobre 2020.**   *Today is the first of October, 2020.*

Repeat :   **Nous sommes le premier octobre 2020.**   *Today is the first of October, 2020.*

THE HOURS

Vocabulary

English word	French
word	
An hour	**une heure**
A minute	**une minute**
A second	**une seconde**
A quarter	**un quart**
A half	**une demie**
The morning	**le matin**
The afternoon	**l'après-midi**
The evening	**le soir**
The night	**la nuit**
Noon/midday	**midi**
Midnight	**minuit**

The time	**le temps**
Today	**aujourd'hui**
Yesterday	**hier**
Tomorrow	**demain**

English word	French
word	
A watch	**une montre**
A clock	**une horloge**
Eight o'clock A.M	**huit heures du matin**
Nine o'clock A.M	**neuf heures du matin**
Ten o'clock A.M	**dix heures du matin**
Eleven o'clock A.M	**onze heures du matin**

One o'clock P.M	**treize heures**

Two o'clock P.M	**quatorze heures**

Three o'clock P.M	**quinze heures**

Four o'clock P.M	**seize heures**

Five o'clock P.M	**dix-sept heures**

Six o'clock P.M	**dix-huit heures**

Seven o'clock P.M	**dix-neuf heures**

Eight o'clock P.M	**vingt heures**

Nine o'clock P.M	**vingt-et-une heures**

English word	French word
Ten o'clock P.M	**vingt-deux heures**

English word	French word
Eleven o'clock P.M	**vingt-trois heures**
One o'clock A.M	**une heure du matin**

Dialogs

<u>Dialog 1</u>

What time is it?	**Quelle heure est-il ?**

It's eight o'clock A.M.	**Il est huit heures du matin.**

<u>Dialog 2</u>

When does the train leave? **Quand le train part-il ?**

The train leaves at noon. **Le train part à midi.**

Dialog 3

How long does the exam last? **Combien de temps dure l'examen ?**

It lasts three hours. **Il dure trois heures.**

Dialog 4

When does the lesson start? **Quand commence la leçon ?**

It starts at a quarter to nine. **Elle commence à neuf heures moins le quart.**

Practice

English :   eight o'clock A.M

French :   **huit heures du matin**

Repeat :   **huit heures du matin**

Repeat :   **huit heures du matin**

Spell :   **h-u-i-t-h-e-u-r-e-s-d-u-m-a-t-i-n**

Spell :   **h-u-i-t-h-e-u-r-e-s-d-u-m-a-t-i-n**

In a phrase : **Il est huit heures du matin.**   *It's eight o'clock A.M.*

Repeat : **Il est huit heures du matin.**   *It's eight o'clock A.M.*

Repeat : **Il est huit heures du matin.**   *It's eight o'clock A.M.*

Repeat : **Il est huit heures du matin.**   *It's eight o'clock A.M.*

English :   noon

French :   **midi**

Repeat :   **midi**

Repeat :   **midi**

Spell :   **m-i-d-i**

Spell :   **m-i-d-i**

In a phrase : **Le train part à midi.**   *The train leaves at noon.*

Repeat :   **Le train part à midi.**   *The train leaves at noon.*

Repeat :   **Le train part à midi.**   *The train leaves at noon.*

Repeat :   **Le train part à midi.**   *The train leaves at noon.*

English :   three hours

French :   **trois heures**

Repeat :   **trois heures**

Repeat :   **trois heures**

Spell :   **t-h-r-e-e-h-o-u-r-s**

Spell :   **t-h-r-e-e-h-o-u-r-s**

In a phrase : **Il dure trois heures.**   *It lasts three hours.*

Repeat :   **Il dure trois heures.**   *It lasts three hours.*

Repeat :   **Il dure trois heures.**   *It lasts three hours.*

Repeat :   **Il dure trois heures.**   *It lasts three hours.*

English :   a quarter to nine

French :   **neuf heures moins le quart**

Repeat :   **neuf heures moins le quart**

Repeat :   **neuf heures moins le quart**

Spell :   **n-e-u-f-h-e-u-r-e-s-m-o-i-n-s-l-e-q-u-a-r-t**

Spell :   **n-e-u-f-h-e-u-r-e-s-m-o-i-n-s-l-e-q-u-a-r-t**

In a phrase : **Elle commence à neuf heures moins le quart.**   *It starts at a quarter to nine.*

Repeat : **Elle commence à neuf heures moins le quart.** *It starts at a quarter to nine.*

Repeat : **Elle commence à neuf heures moins le quart.** *It starts at a quarter to nine.*

Repeat : **Elle commence à neuf heures moins le quart.** *It starts at a quarter to nine.*

GREETINGS

Vocabulary

English word	French word
Mister / Mr	**Monsieur / M**
Misses / Mrs	**Madame / Mme**
Miss	**Mademoiselle / Mlle**
Good day!	**Bonjour !**
Good morning!	**Bonjour !**
Good afternoon!	**Bonjour !**
Good evening!	**Bonsoir !**
Good night / night!	**Bonne nuit !**
Hello / Hi!	**Salut !**
Hello (close friends)!	**Coucou !**
Have a nice day!	**Bonne journée !**
Have a nice evening!	**Bonne soirée !**

See you later! **À plus tard !**

See you soon! **À bientôt!**

See you tomorrow! **À demain !**

See you next year! **À l'année prochaine !**

See you! **À plus !**

Good bye! **Au revoir !**

Bye-bye! **Bye !**

Thank you **Merci**

Thank you very much **Merci beaucoup**

<u>English word word</u>   <u>French</u>

Please **S'il te plait**

Please (formal) **S'il vous plaît**

Pleasure to meet you **enchanté(e)**

How are you? **Comment vas-tu ?**

How are you? **Ça va ?**

I'm fine. **Je vais bien.**

Well **bien**

Very well **très bien**

Not too bad **pas trop mal**

So-so **bof**

Not good **pas bien**

What's your name? **Comment tu t'appelles ?**

My name is... **Je m'appelle...**

Happy to meet you. **Content de faire ta connaissance**

I'd like you to meet **Je vous présente**

Happy birthday! **Joyeux anniversaire !**

Merry Christmas! **Joyeux Noël !**

Happy New Year! **Bonne année !**

Best wishes! **Meilleurs voeux !**

Congratulations! **Félicitations !**

Dialogs

Dialog 1

Good morning Mary, welcome in our school! **Bonjour Mary, bienvenue dans notre école !**

Good morning Mrs Stanford. **Bonjour Madame Stanford.**

Dialog 2

How are you today, Mary? **Comment vas-tu aujourd'hui, Mary ?**

I'm fine, thank you. **Je vais bien, merci.**

Dialog 3

Can you give me this book, please? **Peux-tu me donner ce livre, s'il te plaît ?**

Sure, here is the book. **Voici le livre.**

<u>Dialog 4</u>

I will see you tomorrow, bye. **Je vous reverrai demain, au revoir.**

Bye! See you tomorrow! **Au revoir ! À demain !**

Practice

English : good morning

French : **bonjour**

Repeat : **bonjour**

Repeat : **bonjour**

Spell : **b-o-n-j-o-u-r**

Spell : **b-o-n-j-o-u-r**

In a phrase : **Bonjour Madame Stanford.** *Good morning, Mrs Stanford.*

Repeat : **Bonjour Madame Stanford.** *Good morning, Mrs Stanford.*

Repeat : **Bonjour Madame Stanford.** *Good morning, Mrs Stanford.*

Repeat : **Bonjour Madame Stanford.** *Good morning, Mrs Stanford.*

English :   fine

French :   **bien**

Repeat :   **bien**

Repeat :   **bien**

Spell :   **b-i-e-n**

Spell :   **b-i-e-n**

In a phrase :   **Je vais bien, merci.**   *I'm fine, thank you.*

Repeat :   **Je vais bien, merci.**   *I'm fine, thank you.*

Repeat :   **Je vais bien, merci.**   *I'm fine, thank you.*

Repeat :   **Je vais bien, merci.**   *I'm fine, thank you.*

English :   please

French :   **s'il te plaît**

Repeat :   **s'il te plaît**

Repeat :   **s'il te plaît**

Spell :   **s-i-l-t-e-p-l-a-î-t**

Spell :   **s-i-l-t-e-p-l-a-î-t**

In a phrase :   **Peux-tu me donner ce livre, s'il te plaît ?**   *Can you give me this book, please?*

Repeat :   **Peux-tu me donner ce livre, s'il te plaît ?**   *Can you give me this book, please?*

Repeat :   **Peux-tu me donner ce livre, s'il te plaît ?**   *Can you give me this book, please?*

Repeat :   **Peux-tu me donner ce livre, s'il te plaît ?**   *Can you give me this book, please?*

English :   bye

French :   **au revoir**

Repeat :   **au revoir**

Repeat :   **au revoir**

Spell :   **a-u-r-e-v-o-i-r**

Spell :   **a-u-r-e-v-o-i-r**

In a phrase :   **Au revoir ! À demain !**   *Bye! See you tomorrow!*

Repeat :   **Au revoir ! À demain !**   *Bye! See you tomorrow!*

Repeat :   **Au revoir ! À demain !**   *Bye! See you tomorrow!*

Repeat :   **Au revoir ! À demain !**   *Bye! See you tomorrow!*

Chapter 2: TALKING ABOUT ME

The first elements you mention when you speak is your everyday life and you generally talk about you. There is a useful basic vocabulary list you need to know if you talk about yourself, linked to your physical appearance or your emotions. Let's discover how you can talk about yourself in French!

PEOPLE AND TIME

Vocabulary

English word word	French
A man	**un homme**
A woman	**une femme**
A baby	**un bébé**
A child	**un enfant**
A teenager	**un adolescent**
A young	**un jeune**
An adult	**un adulte**
A working person	**un actif**
A retired person	**un retraité**
An unemployed	**un chômeur**
A disabled	**un handicapé**

A pregnant woman	**une femme enceinte**
An injured person	**une personne blessée**
An old person	**une personne âgée**
The youngs	**les jeunes**
The elderly	**les personnes âgées**

<u>English word</u>	<u>French</u>
word	
Birth	**la naissance**
Teenaghood	**l'adolescence**
Childhood	**la jeunesse**
Adulthood	**l'âge adulte**
Retirement	**le retraite**

The old age	**la vieillesse**
Be born	**naître**
Grow up	**grandir**
Leave home	**quitter la maison**
To work	**travailler**
To move out	**déménager**
To go on holidays	**partir en vacances**
To hurt oneself	**se faire mal**
Be pregnant	**être enceinte**
To go on retirement	**partir à la retraite**
To die	**mourir**
To pass away	**décéder**

Dialogs

<u>Dialog 1</u>

Can you drive?   **Sais-tu conduire ?**

No, I'm just a teenager.   **Non, je ne suis qu'un adolescent.**

<u>Dialog 2</u>

Do you want to go there?   **Veux-tu aller là-bas ?**

No, only adults are allowed there.   **Non, seuls les adultes y sont autorisés.**

<u>Dialog 3</u>

Is your mother at home?   **Ta mère est-elle à la maison ?**

No, she is an active woman.   **Non, c'est une femme active.**

<u>Dialog 4</u>

Where were you born?   **Où es-tu né ?**

I was born in England.   **Je suis né en Angleterre.**

Practice

English :   teenager

French :   **adolescent**

Repeat :   **adolescent**

Repeat :   **adolescent**

Spell :   **a-d-o-l-e-s-c-e-n-t**

Spell :   **a-d-o-l-e-s-c-e-n-t**

In a phrase : **Non, je ne suis qu'un adolescent.** *No, I'm only a teenager.*

Repeat :   **Non, je ne suis qu'un adolescent.** *No, I'm only a teenager.*

Repeat :   **Non, je ne suis qu'un adolescent.** *No, I'm only a teenager.*

Repeat :   **Non, je ne suis qu'un adolescent.** *No, I'm only a teenager.*

English :   adult

French :   **adulte**

Repeat :   **adulte**

Repeat :   **adulte**

Spell :   **a-d-u-l-t-e**

Spell :   **a-d-u-l-t-e**

In a phrase :   **Non, seuls les adultes y sont autorisés.**   *No, only adults are allowed there.*

Repeat :   **Non, seuls les adultes y sont autorisés.**   *No, only adults are allowed there.*

Repeat :   **Non, seuls les adultes y sont autorisés.**   *No, only adults are allowed there.*

Repeat :   **Non, seuls les adultes y sont autorisés.**   *No, only adults are allowed there.*

English :   woman

French :   **femme**

Repeat :   **femme**

Repeat :   **femme**

Spell :   **f-e-m-m-e**

Spell :   **f-e-m-m-e**

In a phrase :   **Non, c'est une femme active.**   *No, she is an active woman.*

Repeat :   **Non, c'est une femme active.**   *No, she is an active woman.*

Repeat :   **Non, c'est une femme active.**   *No, she is an active woman.*

Repeat :   **Non, c'est une femme active.**   *No, she is an active woman.*

English :   I was born

French :   **Je suis né**

Repeat :   **Je suis né**

Repeat :   **Je suis né**

Spell :   **j-e-s-u-i-s-n-é**

Spell :   **j-e-s-u-i-s-n-é**

In a phrase : **Je suis né en Angleterre.** *I was born in England.*

Repeat :   **Je suis né en Angleterre.** *I was born in England.*

Repeat :   **Je suis né en Angleterre.** *I was born in England.*

Repeat :   **Je suis né en Angleterre.** *I was born in England.*

THE HUMAN BODY

Vocabulary

English word word	French
The body	**le corps**

English word word	French
The head	**la tête**
The face	**le visage**
The hair	**les cheveux**
The forehead	**le front**
The eyebrows	**les sourcils**
The eye	**l'oeil**
The eyes	**les yeux**
The eyelashes	**les cils**
The eyelids	**les paupières**

The ears	**les oreilles**
The nose	**le nez**
The cheeks	**les pommettes**
The mouth	**la bouche**
The lip	**la lèvre**
The tooth	**la dent**
The teeth	**les dents**
The chin	**le menton**
The jaw	**la machoire**
The neck	**le cou**
The shoulder	**l'épaule**
The bust	**le buste**
The chest	**la poitrine**

The arm	**le bras**	The bottom	**les fesses**
The forearm	**l'avant-bras**	The thigh	**la cuisse**
The wrist	**le poignet**	The leg	**la jambe**
The hand	**la main**	The knee	**le genou**
The finger	**le doigt**	The calf	**le mollet**
The thumb	**le pouce**	The ankle	**la cheville**
The nail	**l'ongle**	The foot	**le pied**
The belly	**le ventre**	The heel	**le talon**
The hips	**les hanches**	The toe	**l'orteil**

Dialogs

<u>Dialog 1</u>

Wash your hands before going to eat! **Lave-toi les mains avant d'aller manger.**

Yes mum. **Oui maman.**

<u>Dialog 2</u>

Where does it hurt? **Où as-tu mal ?**

I can't move my leg. **Je ne peux pas bouger la jambe.**

<u>Dialog 3</u>

What does he look like? **À quoi ressemble-t-il ?**

He has big eyes and a small nose. **Il a de grands yeux et un petit nez.**

<u>Dialog 4</u>

Please try these shoes. **Veux-tu essayer ces chaussures.**

I can't, my feet are too big. **Je ne peux pas, mes pieds sont trop grands.**

English : hand

French : **main**

Repeat : **main**

Repeat : **main**

Spell : **m-a-i-n**

Spell : **m-a-i-n**

In a phrase : **Lave-toi les mains avant d'aller manger.**
Wash your hands before going to eat.

Repeat : **Lave-toi les mains avant d'aller manger.**
Wash your hands before going to eat.

Repeat : **Lave-toi les mains avant d'aller manger.**
Wash your hands before going to eat.

Repeat : **Lave-toi les mains avant d'aller manger.**
Wash your hands before going to eat.

English : leg

French : **jambe**

Repeat : **jambe**

Repeat : **jambe**

Spell : **j-a-m-b-e**

Spell : **j-a-m-b-e**

In a phrase : **Je ne peux pas bouger la jambe.** *I can't move my leg.*

Repeat : **Je ne peux pas bouger la jambe.** *I can't move my leg.*

Repeat : **Je ne peux pas bouger la jambe.** *I can't move my leg.*

Repeat :   **Je ne peux pas bouger la jambe.**   *I can't move my leg.*

English :   nose

French :   **nez**

Repeat :   **nez**

Repeat :   **nez**

Spell :   **n-e-z**

Spell :   **n-e-z**

In a phrase :   **Il a de grands yeux et un petit nez.**   *He has big eyes and a small nose.*

Repeat :   **Il a de grands yeux et un petit nez.**   *He has big eyes and a small nose.*

Repeat :   **Il a de grands yeux et un petit nez.**   *He has big eyes and a small nose.*

Repeat :   **Il a de grands yeux et un petit nez.**   *He has big eyes and a small nose.*

English :   feet

French :   **pieds**

Repeat :   **pieds**

Repeat :   **pieds**

Spell :   **p-i-e-d-s**

Spell :   **p-i-e-d-s**

In a phrase :   **Je ne peux pas, mes pieds sont trop grands.**   *I can't, my feet are too big.*

Repeat :   **Je ne peux pas, mes pieds sont trop grands.**   *I can't, my feet are too big.*

Repeat :   **Je ne peux pas, mes pieds sont trop grands.**   *I can't, my feet are too big.*

Repeat :   **Je ne peux pas, mes pieds sont trop grands.**   *I can't, my feet are too big.*

PHYSICAL DESCRIPTION

Vocabulary

English word word	French		
Very tall	**très grand**	Obese	**obèse**
		Stout	**corpulent**
Tall	**grand**	Plump	**dodu**
Small	**petit**	Overweight	**en surpoids**
Medium-sized	**de taille-moyenne**	Normal	**de poids normal**

Slender **élancé**

Muscular **musclé**

Thin **svelte**

Slim **mince**

Skinny **maigre**

Blond **blond**

Brown **brun**

Red, ginger **roux**

English word word	French
Fair	**clair**
Dark	**foncé**
Grey	**gris**

Short hair **cheveux courts**

Medium-length **mi-long**

Long **long**

Straight **raide**

Wavy **ondulé**

Curled **bouclé**

Frizzy **frisé**

A plait **une tresse**

A bun **un chignon**

A pony tail **une queue de cheval**

blue eyes **les yeux bleus**

A crooked nose **un nez crochu**

A pointed nose **un nez pointu**

A moustache **une moustache**

English word word	French
A beard	**une barbe**
Bald	**chauve**

Baldness	**La calvitie**	A spot	**un bouton**
White skin	**La peau blanche**	A scar	**une cicatrice**
Light	**clair**	A birth mark	**une marque de naissance**
Tanned	**bronzé**	Good-looking	**mignon**
Dark	**foncé**	Beautiful, handsome	**beau, belle**
Mixed-race	**métisse**	Pretty, attractive	**jolie**
A wrinkle	**une ride**	Ugly	**laid, moche**
A freckle	**une tache de rousseur**	Plain	**banal**

Dialog

<u>Dialog 1</u>

What does he look like? **À quoi ressemble-t-il ?**

He is a tall and slender man. **C'est un homme grand et élancé.**

<u>Dialog 2</u>

Do you like her hair? **Aimes-tu ses cheveux ?**

Yes, she has red and curly hair. **Oui, elle
a les cheveux roux et bouclés.**

Dialog 3

What an amazing glaze! **Quel incroyable
regard !**

Yes, he has impressive blue eyes. **Oui, il a des
yeux bleus impressionnants.**

Dialog 4

How did you recognize her? **Comment l'as-
tu reconnu ?**

She has freckles. **Elle a des
taches de rousseur.**

Practice

English :   tall

French :   **grand**

Repeat :   **grand**

Repeat :   **grand**

Spell :   **g-r-a-n-d**

Spell :   **g-r-a-n-d**

In a phrase :   **C'est un homme grand et élancé.**   *He is a tall and slender man.*

Repeat :   **C'est un homme grand et élancé.**   *He is a tall and slender man.*

Repeat :   **C'est un homme grand et élancé.**   *He is a tall and slender man.*

Repeat :   **C'est un homme grand et élancé.**   *He is a tall and slender man.*

English :   ginger

French :   **roux**

Repeat :   **roux**

Repeat :   **roux**

Spell :   **r-o-u-x**

Spell :   **r-o-u-x**

In a phrase :   **Oui, elle a les cheveux roux et bouclés.**   *Yes, she has ginger and curly hair.*

Repeat :   **Oui, elle a les cheveux roux et bouclés.**   *Yes, she has ginger and curly hair.*

Repeat :   **Oui, elle a les cheveux roux et bouclés.**   *Yes, she has ginger and curly hair.*

Repeat :   **Oui, elle a les cheveux roux et bouclés.**   *Yes, she has ginger and curly hair.*

English :   eyes

French :   **yeux**

Repeat :   **yeux**

Repeat :   **yeux**

Spell :   **y-e-u-x**

Spell :   **y-e-u-x**

In a phrase : **Oui, il a des yeux bleus impressionnants.**   *Yes, he has impressive blue eyes.*

Repeat :   **Oui, il a des yeux bleus impressionnants.**   *Yes, he has impressive blue eyes.*

Repeat :   **Oui, il a des yeux bleus impressionnants.**   *Yes, he has impressive blue eyes.*

Repeat :   **Oui, il a des yeux bleus impressionnants.**   *Yes, he has impressive blue eyes.*

English :   freckles

French :   **taches de rousseur**

Repeat :   **taches de rousseur**

Repeat :   **taches de rousseur**

Spell :   **t-a-c-h-e-s-d-e-r-o-u-s-s-e-u-r**

Spell :   **t-a-c-h-e-s-d-e-r-o-u-s-s-e-u-r**

In a phrase : **Elle a des taches de rousseur.**   *She has freckles.*

Repeat :   **Elle a des taches de rousseur.**   *She has freckles.*

Repeat :   **Elle a des taches de rousseur.**   *She has freckles.*

Repeat :   **Elle a des taches de rousseur.**   *She has freckles.*

CLOTHES

Vocabulary

English word word	French		
		A top	**un haut, débardeur**
A pullover	**un pullover**	A t-shirt	**un t-shirt**
A sweater	**un sweat**	A body	**un body**
A cardigan	**un gilet**	Trousers, pants	**un pantalon**

Jeans	**un jean**
<u>English word</u> word	<u>French</u>
Capri-pants	**un pantacourt**
A shirt	**une chemise**
A blouse	**un chemisier**
A dress	**une robe**
A skirt	**une jupe**
Overalls	**une salopette**
A suit	**une combinaison**
Tights	**des collants**
<u>English word</u> word	<u>French</u>
Socks	**des chaussettes**

Underpants	**un slip**
A bra	**un soutien-gorge**
An underwear	**un sous-vêtement**
A coat	**un manteau**
A jacket	**une veste**
A raincoat	**un k-way**
Shoes	**des chaussures**
Boots	**des bottes**
<u>English word</u> word	<u>French</u>
High-heeled-shoes	**des escarpins**
Sneakers	**des tennis**
Slippers	**des chaussons**

A hat	**un chapeau**	A tie	**une cravate**
A wolly hat	**un bonnet**	A bow-tie	**un noeud-papillon**
A scarf	**une écharpe**	A belt	**une ceinture**
Gloves	**des gants**		

Dialogs

<u>Dialog 1</u>

What is she wearing today? **Que porte-t-elle aujourd'hui ?**

She is wearing a blue dress. **Elle porte une robe bleue.**

<u>Dialog 2</u>

Have you seen my coat? **As-tu vu mon manteau ?**

I cleaned your coat; it is still wet! **J'ai nettoyé ton manteau, il est toujours mouillé.**

<u>Dialog 3</u>

It's raining a lot outside. **Il pleut beaucoup dehors.**

Take off your shoes, the house is clean. **Enlève tes chaussures, la maison est propre.**

<u>Dialog 4</u>

She never wears any pants. **Elle ne porte jamais de pantalon.**

Yes, she wanted a new style. **Oui, elle voulait un nouveau style.**

Practice

English : dress

French : **robe**

Repeat : **robe**

Repeat : **robe**

Spell : **r-o-b-e**

Spell : **r-o-b-e**

In a phrase : **Elle porte une robe bleue.** *She is wearing a blue dress.*

Repeat : **Elle porte une robe bleue.** *She is wearing a blue dress.*

Repeat : **Elle porte une robe bleue.** *She is wearing a blue dress.*

Repeat :   **Elle porte une robe bleue.**   *She is wearing a blue dress.*

English :   coat

French :   **manteau**

Repeat :   **manteau**

Repeat :   **manteau**

Spell :   **m-a-n-t-e-a-u**

Spell :   **m-a-n-t-e-a-u**

In a phrase :   **As-tu vu mon manteau ?**   *Have you seen my coat?*

Repeat :   **As-tu vu mon manteau ?**   *Have you seen my coat?*

Repeat :   **As-tu vu mon manteau ?**   *Have you seen my coat?*

Repeat :   **As-tu vu mon manteau ?**   *Have you seen my coat?*

English :   shoes

French :   **chaussures**

Repeat :   **chaussures**

Repeat : **chaussures**

Spell : **c-h-a-u-s-s-u-r-e-s**

Spell : **c-h-a-u-s-s-u-r-e-s**

In a phrase : **Enlève tes chaussures, la maison est propre.**
Take off your shoes, the house is clean.

Repeat : **Enlève tes chaussures, la maison est propre.**
Take off your shoes, the house is clean.

Repeat : **Enlève tes chaussures, la maison est propre.**
Take off your shoes, the house is clean.

Repeat : **Enlève tes chaussures, la maison est propre.**
Take off your shoes, the house is clean.

English : pants

French : **pantalon**

Repeat : **pantalon**

Repeat : **pantalon**

Spell : **p-a-n-t-a-l-o-n**

Spell : **p-a-n-t-a-l-o-n**

In a phrase : **Elle ne porte jamais de pantalon.** *She never wears any pants.*

Repeat :   **Elle ne porte jamais de pantalon.** *She never wears any pants.*

Repeat :   **Elle ne porte jamais de pantalon.** *She never wears any pants.*

Repeat :   **Elle ne porte jamais de pantalon.** *She never wears any pants.*

PERSONALITY TRAITS

Vocabulary

English word word	French
Friendly	**amical**
Attentive	**attentif**
Caring	**attentionné**
Good-willing	**bonne volonté**
Brilliant	**brillant**
Calm	**calme**
Captivating	**captivant**
Confident	**confiant**
Hearty	**chaleureux**
Charismatic	**charismatique**
Courageous	**courageux**
Curious	**curieux**
Dedicated	**dévoué**
Witty	**drôle**

Dynamic, lively **dynamique**

Educated **éduqué**

<u>English word</u> <u>French word</u>

Balanced **equilibré**

Stubborn **entêté**

Enthusiastic **enthousiaste**

Reliable **fiable**

Strong **fort**

Cheerful **gai**

Kind, nice **gai**

Generous **généreux**

Grumpy **grincheux**

Idealistic **idéaliste**

Impressive **impressionnant**

Forgiving **indulgent**

Innovative **innovant**

Clever, bright **intelligent**

Skilful **habile**

Fair, faithful **loyal**

<u>English word</u> <u>French word</u>

Bad **méchant**

Painstaking **méticuleux**

Humble, modest **modeste**

Optimistic **optimiste**

Peaceful **paisible**

Lazy **paresseux**

Patriotic **patriotique**

Pessimistic
pessimiste

Popular
populaire

Practical
pratique

Prudent
prudent

English word	French
word	
Realistic	**réaliste**
Reserved	**reservé**
Dutiful,	respectful
respecteux	

Romantic
romantique

Wise   **sage**

Helpful
serviable

Earnest
sincère

Sociable
sociable

Cheeky
taquin

Shy   **timide**

Hard-working
travailleur

Genuine   **vrai**

Dialog

<u>Dialog 1</u>

How could he do this?
Comment a-t-il pu le faire ?

Don't be surprised, he is a bright man!   **Ne sois pas surpris, c'est un homme intelligent !**

<u>Dialog 2</u>

Why don't you come with us? **Pourquoi
ne viens-tu pas avec nous ?**

I'm too shy to do this! **Je suis trop
timide pour le faire !**

Dialog 3

He has already finished! **Il a déjà fini !**

Yes, he is a hardworking man! **Oui, c'est
un travailleur !**

Dialog 4

Should I work with John? **Devrais-je
travailler avec John ?**

Yes, he is reliable. **Oui, c'est
quelqu'un de fiable.**

Practice

English :   clever

French :   **intelligent**

Repeat :   **intelligent**

Repeat :   **intelligent**

Spell :   **i-n-t-e-l-l-i-g-e-n-t**

Spell :   **i-n-t-e-l-l-i-g-e-n-t**

In a phrase :   **C'est un homme intelligent !** *He is a clever man.*

Repeat :   **C'est un homme intelligent !** *He is a clever man.*

Repeat :   **C'est un homme intelligent !** *He is a clever man.*

Repeat :   **C'est un homme intelligent !** *He is a clever man.*

English :   shy

French :   **timide**

Repeat :   **timide**

Repeat :   **timide**

Spell :   **t-i-m-i-d-e**

Spell :   **t-i-m-i-d-e**

In a phrase :   **Je suis trop timide pour le faire !** *I'm too shy to do it!*

Repeat :   **Je suis trop timide pour le faire !** *I'm too shy to do it!*

Repeat :   **Je suis trop timide pour le faire !** *I'm too shy to do it!*

Repeat :   **Je suis trop timide pour le faire !** *I'm too shy to do it!*

English :   hard-working

French :   **travailleur**

Repeat :   **travailleur**

Repeat :   **travailleur**

Spell :   **t-r-a-v-a-i-l-l-e-u-r**

Spell :   **t-r-a-v-a-i-l-l-e-u-r**

In a phrase :   **Oui, c'est un travailleur !** *Yes, he is a hardworking man.*

Repeat :   **Oui, c'est un travailleur !** *Yes, he is a hardworking man.*

Repeat :   **Oui, c'est un travailleur !** *Yes, he is a hardworking man.*

Repeat :   **Oui, c'est un travailleur !** *Yes, he is a hardworking man.*

English :   reliable

French :   **fiable**

Repeat :   **fiable**

Repeat :   **fiable**

Spell :   **f-i-a-b-l-e**

Spell :   **f-i-a-b-l-e**

In a phrase : **Oui, c'est quelqu'un de fiable.** *Yes, he is reliable.*

Repeat :   **Oui, c'est quelqu'un de fiable.** *Yes, he is reliable.*

Repeat :   **Oui, c'est quelqu'un de fiable.** *Yes, he is reliable.*

Repeat :   **Oui, c'est quelqu'un de fiable.** *Yes, he is reliable.*

EMOTIONS

Vocabulary

English word word	French		
		Bitter	**amer**
		In love	**amoureux**
Crushed	**accablé**		
Agitated	**agité**	Amused	**amusé**
Ambitious	**ambitieux**	Calm	**calme**

English word	French
Confident	**confiant**
Confused	**confus**
Happy	**content**
Upset, annoyed	**contrarié**
Creative	**créatif**
Disgusted	**dégouté**
Depressed	**déprimé**

English word word	French
Desperate	**désespéré**
Determined	**determiné**
Hateful	**détestable**
Amazed	**ébahi**
Embarrassed	**embarrassé**
Angry	**énervé**
Joyful	**enjoué**

English word	French
Enthousiastic	**enthousiaste**
Emotional	**émotif**
Astonished	**étonné**
Tired	**fatigué**
Mad	**fou**
Frustrated	**frustré**
Annoyed	**gêné**

English word word	French
Glad	**heureux**
Uncertain	**incertain**
Outraged	**indigné**
Bold	**intrépide**
Joyful	**joyeux**
Nervous	**nerveux**

| Hardy | **osé** |
| Delighted | **réjoui** |

<u>English word</u>	<u>French word</u>
Lost	**perdu**
Tenacious	**perseverant**
Powerful	**puissant**

Resentful **rancunier**

Grateful **reconnaissant**

Healthy **sain, solide**

Pleased **satisfait**

Surprised **surpris**

Sad, mourneful **triste**

Dialogs

<u>Dialog 1</u>

Why is he so dizzy? **Pourquoi est-il si étourdi ?**

He is in love. **Il est amoureux.**

<u>Dialog 2</u>

What is happening? **Que se passe-t-il ?**

I'm so glad, we won. **Je suis si heureux, nous avons gagné.**

<u>Dialog 3</u>

I'm very happy today. **Je suis très content aujourd'hui.**

I've noticed that. **Je l'ai remarqué.**

<u>Dialog 4</u>

Why are you so upset? **Pourquoi es-tu si contrarié ?**

I'm upset because of the weather. **Je suis contrarié à cause du temps.**

Practice

English :   in love

French :   **amoureux**

Repeat :   **amoureux**

Repeat :   **amoureux**

Spell :   **a-m-o-u-r-e-u-x**

Spell :   **a-m-o-u-r-e-u-x**

In a phrase : **Il est amoureux.** *He is in love.*

Repeat : **Il est amoureux.** *He is in love.*

Repeat : **Il est amoureux.** *He is in love.*

Repeat :	**Il est amoureux.** *He is in love.*

English :	glad
French :	**heureux**
Repeat :	**heureux**
Repeat :	**heureux**
Spell :	**h-e-u-r-e-u-x**
Spell :	**h-e-u-r-e-u-x**

In a phrase :	**Je suis si heureux.** *I'm so glad.*
Repeat :	**Je suis si heureux.** *I'm so glad.*
Repeat :	**Je suis si heureux.** *I'm so glad.*
Repeat :	**Je suis si heureux.** *I'm so glad.*

English :	happy
French :	**content**
Repeat :	**content**
Repeat :	**content**
Spell :	**c-o-n-t-e-n-t**
Spell :	**c-o-n-t-e-n-t**

In a phrase :   **Je suis très content aujourd'hui.** *I'm very happy today.*

Repeat :   **Je suis très content aujourd'hui.** *I'm very happy today.*

Repeat :   **Je suis très content aujourd'hui.** *I'm very happy today.*

Repeat :   **Je suis très content aujourd'hui.** *I'm very happy today.*

English :   upset

French :   **contrarié**

Repeat :   **contrarié**

Repeat :   **contrarié**

Spell :   **c-o-n-t-r-a-r-i-é**

Spell :   **c-o-n-t-r-a-r-i-é**

In a phrase :   **Pourquoi es-tu si contrarié ?** *Why are you so upset?*

Repeat :   **Pourquoi es-tu si contrarié ?** *Why are you so upset?*

Repeat :   **Pourquoi es-tu si contrarié ?** *Why are you so upset?*

Repeat :   **Pourquoi es-tu si contrarié ?** *Why are you so upset?*

Chapter 3: PEOPLE AROUND ME

Talking about your everyday life or talking everyday implies discussions with people around you. It may be members of your family, relatives or people you usually meet. Let's review their name in French.

MY FAMILY

Vocabulary

English word word	French
The father	**le père**
The mother	**la mère**
The brother	**le frère**
The sister	**la sœur**
The younger brother	**le petit frère**
The younger sister	**la petite sœur**
The older brother	**le grand frère**
The older sister	**la grande sœur**
The step-brother	**le demi-frère**
The brother-in-law	**le demi-frère**
The cousin	**le cousin**
The father-in-law	**le beau-père**
The mother-in-law	**la belle-mère**
The grand-father	**le grand-père**

The grand-mother   **la grand-mère**

The uncle   **l'oncle**

The aunt   **la tante**

The nephew   **le neveu**

The niece   **la nièce**

The son   **le fils**

The daughter   **la fille**

The grand-son   **le petit-fils**

The grand-daughter   **la petite fille**

The relatives   **les proches**

Dialogs

<u>Dialog 1</u>

You look like your mother!   **Tu ressembles à ta mère !**

Everybody says so.   **Tout le monde le dit.**

<u>Dialog 2</u>

I have broken a glass.   **J'ai cassé un verre.**

Like father, like son!   **Tel père, tel fils !**

<u>Dialog 3</u>

Where is your sister?   **Où est ta soeur ?**

She is out with her friends. **Elle est sortie avec des amis.**

<u>Dialog 4</u>

Do you have brothers and sisters? **As-tu des frères et sœurs ?**

I only have a step-brother. **Je n'ai qu'un demi-frère.**

Practice

English :   mother

French :   **mère**

Repeat :   **mère**

Repeat :   **mère**

Spell :   **m-è-r-e**

Spell :   **m-è-r-e**

In a phrase : **Tu ressembles à ta mère !** *You look like your mother!*

Repeat :   **Tu ressembles à ta mère !** *You look like your mother!*

Repeat :   **Tu ressembles à ta mère !** *You look like your mother!*

Repeat :   **Tu ressembles à ta mère !**   *You look like your mother!*

English :   father

French :   **père**

Repeat :   **père**

Repeat :   **père**

Spell :   **p-è-r-e**

Spell :   **p-è-r-e**

In a phrase :   **Tel père, tel fils !**   *Like father, like son!*

Repeat :   **Tel père, tel fils !**   *Like father, like son!*

Repeat :   **Tel père, tel fils !**   *Like father, like son!*

Repeat :   **Tel père, tel fils !**   *Like father, like son!*

English :   sister

French :   **soeur**

Repeat :   **soeur**

Repeat :   **soeur**

Spell :   **s-o-e-u-r**

Spell :   s-**o-e-u-r**

In a phrase : **Où est ta soeur?** *Where is your sister?*

Repeat : **Où est ta soeur?** *Where is your sister?*

Repeat : **Où est ta soeur?** *Where is your sister?*

Repeat : **Où est ta soeur?** *Where is your sister?*

English : step-brother

French : **demi-frère**

Repeat : **demi-frère**

Repeat : **demi-frère**

Spell : **d-e-m-i-f-r-è-r-e**

Spell : **d-e-m-i-f-r-è-r-e**

In a phrase : **Je n'ai qu'un demi-frère.** *I only have a step-brother.*

Repeat : **Je n'ai qu'un demi-frère.** *I only have a step-brother.*

Repeat : **Je n'ai qu'un demi-frère.** *I only have a step-brother.*

Repeat : **Je n'ai qu'un demi-frère.** *I only have a step-brother.*

PEOPLE AT SCHOOL

Vocabulary

English word word	French	English word word	French
The friend	**l'ami**	The supervisory pers.	**le surveillant**
The relative	**la connaissance**	The team	**l'équipe**
The headmaster	**le directeur**	The teacher	**le professeur**
The caterer	**le cantinier**	The secretary	**la secrétaire**
		The nurse	**l'infirmière**

Dialogs

<u>Dialog 1</u>

The teacher said I should study. **Le professeur a dit que je devrais travailler.**

Then go to your room. **Alors va dans ta chambre.**

<u>Dialog 2</u>

I have cheated and can't go to the cinema. **J'ai triché et je ne peux pas aller au cinéma.**

You must have seen the headmaster. **Tu as dû voir le directeur.**

<u>Dialog 3</u>

The nurse said I should stay at home. **L'infirmière a dit que je devrais rester à la maison.**

I know, I just called your mother. **Je sais, je viens juste d'appeler ta mère.**

<u>Dialog 4</u>

My friend told me the lesson is cancelled. **Mon ami m'a dit que le cours est annulé.**

Yes, you have P.E. instead. **Oui, tu as sport à la place.**

Practice

English :   teacher

French :   **professeur**

Repeat :   **professeur**

Repeat :   **professeur**

Spell :   **p-r-o-f-e-s-s-e-u-r**

Spell :   **p-r-o-f-e-s-s-e-u-r**

In a phrase :   **Le professeur a dit que je devrais travailler**
The teacher said I should study.

Repeat :   **Le professeur a dit que je devrais travailler**
The teacher said I should study.

Repeat :   **Le professeur a dit que je devrais travailler**
The teacher said I should study.

Repeat :   **Le professeur a dit que je devrais travailler**
The teacher said I should study.

English :   headmaster

French :   **directeur**

Repeat :   **directeur**

Repeat :   **directeur**

Spell :   **d-i-r-e-c-t-e-u-r**

Spell :   **d-i-r-e-c-t-e-u-r**

In a phrase :   **Tu as dû voir le directeur.** *You must have seen
the headmaster.*

Repeat :   **Tu as dû voir le directeur.** *You must have seen
the headmaster.*

Repeat :   **Tu as dû voir le directeur.** *You must have seen
the headmaster.*

Repeat :   **Tu as dû voir le directeur.** *You must have seen the headmaster.*

English :   nurse

French :   **infirmière**

Repeat :   **infirmière**

Repeat :   **infirmière**

Spell :   **i-n-f-i-r-m-i-è-r-e**

Spell :   **i-n-f-i-r-m-i-è-r-e**

In a phrase :   **L'infirmière a dit que je devrais rester à la maison.** *The nurse said I should stay at home.*

Repeat :   **L'infirmière a dit que je devrais rester à la maison.** *The nurse said I should stay at home.*

Repeat :   **L'infirmière a dit que je devrais rester à la maison.** *The nurse said I should stay at home.*

Repeat :   **L'infirmière a dit que je devrais rester à la maison.** *The nurse said I should stay at home.*

English :   teacher

French :   **professeur**

Repeat :   **professeur**

Repeat :   **professeur**

Spell :   **p-r-o-f-e-s-s-e-u-r**

Spell :   **p-r-o-f-e-s-s-e-u-r**

In a phrase : **Le professeur a dit que je devrais travailler**
The teacher said I should study.

Repeat :   **Le professeur a dit que je devrais travailler**
The teacher said I should study.

Repeat :   **Le professeur a dit que je devrais travailler**
The teacher said I should study.

Repeat :   **Le professeur a dit que je devrais travailler**
The teacher said I should study.

English :   friend

French :   **ami**

Repeat :   **ami**

Repeat :   **ami**

Spell :   **a-m-i**

Spell :   **a-m-i**

In a phrase : **Mon ami m'a dit que le cours est annulé** *My*
friend told me the lesson has been cancelled.

Repeat :   **Mon ami m'a dit que le cours est annulé** *My friend told me the lesson has been cancelled.*

Repeat :   **Mon ami m'a dit que le cours est annulé** *My friend told me the lesson has been cancelled.*

Repeat :   **Mon ami m'a dit que le cours est annulé** *My friend told me the lesson has been cancelled.*

PEOPLE IN TOWN

Vocabulary

English word	French word
The neighbour	**le voisin**
The maid/housekeeper	**la femme de ménage**
The butler	**le majordome**
The boss	**le patron**
The employee	**l'employé**
The worker	**l'ouvrier**
The colleague	**le collègue**
The team	**l'équipe**
The manager	**le chef d'équipe**
The union rep	**le délégué syndical**
The driver	**le chauffeur**
The delivery person	**le livreur**

The postman	**le facteur**	The surgeon	**le chirurgien**
The trader	**le commerçant**	The dentist	**le dentiste**
The baker	**le boulanger**	The chemist	**le pharmacien**
The butcher	**le charcutier**	The jeweller	**le bijoutier**

English word word	French	The bookseller	**le libraire**
The salesman	**le vendeur**	The accountant	**le comptable**
The saleswoman	**la vendeuse**	The hairdresser	**le coiffeur**
The cashier	**la caissière**	The builder	**le constructeur**
The constable	**le gendarme**	The carpenter	**le menuisier**

The policeman	**le policier**	English word word	French
The firefighter	**le pompier**	The chef (cook)	**le chef**
The doctor	**le médecin**	The electrician	**l'électricien**

| The engineer | **l'ingénieur** | The fishmonger | **le poissonnier** |

The plumber | **le plombier**

The receptionist | **le réceptionniste**

The scientist | **le scientifique**

The tailor | **la couturière**

The technician | **le technicien**

The vet | **le vétérinaire**

The waiter | **le serveur**

The waitress | **la serveuse**

The judge | **le juge**

The lawyer | **l'avocat**

The optician | **l'opticien**

The painter | **le peintre**

The photographer | **le photographe**

The welder | **le soudeur**

<u>English word</u> | <u>French word</u>

Dialog

<u>Dialog 1</u>

The neighbour has seen you with a friend. | **Le voisin t'a vu avec un ami.**

Really? He's very curious! | **Vraiment ? Il est très curieux !**

<u>Dialog 2</u>

I haven't seen the postman.	**Je n'ai pas vu le facteur.**
He must be late.	**Il doit être en retard.**

<u>Dialog 3</u>

I can't find the orange juice.	**Je ne trouve pas le jus d'orange.**
You should ask the salesman.	**Tu devrais demander au vendeur.**

<u>Dialog 4</u>

Which job would you like to do later?	**Quel métier aimerais-tu faire plus tard ?**
I would like to become a firefighter.	**J'aimerais devenir pompier.**

Practice

English :   neighbour

French :   **voisin**

Repeat :   **voisin**

Repeat :   **voisin**

Spell :   **v-o-i-s-i-n**

Spell :   **v-o-i-s-i-n**

In a phrase : **Le voisin m'a vu avec un ami.** *The neighbour has seen me with a friend.*

Repeat :   **Le voisin m'a vu avec un ami.** *The neighbour has seen me with a friend.*

Repeat :   **Le voisin m'a vu avec un ami.** *The neighbour has seen me with a friend.*

Repeat :   **Le voisin m'a vu avec un ami.** *The neighbour has seen me with a friend.*

English :   postman

French :   **facteur**

Repeat :   **facteur**

Repeat :   **facteur**

Spell :   **f-a-c-t-e-u-r**

Spell :   **f-a-c-t-e-u-r**

In a phrase : **Je n'ai pas vu le facteur.** *I haven't seen the postman.*

Repeat :   **Je n'ai pas vu le facteur.** *I haven't seen the postman.*

Repeat :   **Je n'ai pas vu le facteur.** *I haven't seen the postman.*

Repeat :   **Je n'ai pas vu le facteur.** *I haven't seen the postman.*

English :   salesman

French :   **vendeur**

Repeat :   **vendeur**

Repeat :   **vendeur**

Spell :   **v-e-n-d-e-u-r**

Spell :   **v-e-n-d-e-u-r**

In a phrase :   **Tu devrais demander au vendeur.** *You should ask the salesman.*

Repeat :   **Tu devrais demander au vendeur.** *You should ask the salesman.*

Repeat :   **Tu devrais demander au vendeur.** *You should ask the salesman.*

Repeat :   **Tu devrais demander au vendeur.** *You should ask the salesman.*

English :   firefighter

French :   **pompier**

Repeat :   **pompier**

Repeat :   **pompier**

Spell :   **p-o-m-p-i-e-r**

Spell :   **p-o-m-p-i-e-r**

In a phrase : **J'aimerais devenir pompier.**   *I would like to become a firefighter.*

Repeat :   **J'aimerais devenir pompier.** *I would like to become a firefighter.*

Repeat :   **J'aimerais devenir pompier.** *I would like to become a firefighter.*

Repeat :   **J'aimerais devenir pompier.** *I would like to become a firefighter.*

ANIMALS

Vocabulary

<u>English word</u>   <u>French</u>   The cat
<u>word</u>   **le chat**

English word	French word	English word	French word
The kitten	**le chaton**	The pony	**le poney**
The dog	**le chien**	The goat	**la chèvre**
The puppy	**le chiot**	The sheep	**le mouton**
The rabbit	**le lapin**	The pig	**le cochon**
The hare	**le lièvre**	The cow	**la vache**
The guinea pig	**le cochon d'inde**	The calf	**le veau**
The turtoise	**la tortue**	The deer	**le cerf**
The fish	**le poisson**	The fox	**le renard**
The bird	**l'oiseau**	The ferret	**le furet**
The parrot	**le perroquet**	The hen	**la poule**
The horse	**le cheval**	The rooster	**le coq**
English word	French word	The chick	**le poussin**

Dialogs

<u>Dialog 1</u>

Have you got a pet?   **As-tu un animal?**

Yes, I have a dog.   **Oui, j'ai un chien.**

<u>Dialog 2</u>

What a mess!   **Quel désordre !**

The cat was alone.   **Le chat était seul.**

<u>Dialog 3</u>

Do you like birds?   **Aimez-vous   les
oiseaux?**

No, I only have a fish.   **Non, je n'ai qu'un
poisson.**

<u>Dialog 4</u>

What are your hobbies?   **Quels   sont   vos
activités ?**

I like going horse riding.   **J'aime   monter   à
cheval.**

Practice

English :   dog

French :   **chien**

Repeat :   **chien**

Repeat :	**chien**
Spell :	**c-h-i-e-n**
Spell :	**c-h-i-e-n**

In a phrase :	**Oui, j'ai un chien.**	*Yes, I have a dog.*
Repeat :	**Oui, j'ai un chien.**	*Yes, I have a dog.*
Repeat :	**Oui, j'ai un chien.**	*Yes, I have a dog.*
Repeat :	**Oui, j'ai un chien.**	*Yes, I have a dog.*

English :	cat
French :	**chat**
Repeat :	**chat**
Repeat :	**chat**
Spell :	**c-h-a-t**
Spell :	**c-h-a-t**

In a phrase :	**Le chat était seul.**	*The cat was alone.*
Repeat :	**Le chat était seul.**	*The cat was alone.*
Repeat :	**Le chat était seul.**	*The cat was alone.*
Repeat :	**Le chat était seul.**	*The cat was alone.*

English :   fish

French :   **poisson**

Repeat :   **poisson**

Repeat :   **poisson**

Spell :   **p-o-i-s-s-o-n**

Spell :   **p-o-i-s-s-o-n**

In a phrase :   **Non, je n'ai qu'un poisson.**   *No, I only have a fish.*

Repeat :   **Non, je n'ai qu'un poisson.**   *No, I only have a fish.*

Repeat :   **Non, je n'ai qu'un poisson.**   *No, I only have a fish.*

Repeat :   **Non, je n'ai qu'un poisson.**   *No, I only have a fish.*

English :   horse

French :   **cheval**

Repeat :   **cheval**

Repeat :   **cheval**

Spell :   **c-h-e-v-a-l**

Spell :   **c-h-e-v-a-l**

In a phrase : **J'aime monter à cheval.**   *I like going horse riding.*

Repeat :   **J'aime monter à cheval.**   *I like going horse riding.*

Repeat :   **J'aime monter à cheval.**   *I like going horse riding.*

Repeat :   **J'aime monter à cheval.**   *I like going horse riding.*

Chapter 4: MY HOBBIES

Talking about your everyday life also means that you will talk about your hobbies -sports or other activities you do during your free time-. Let's review them in French.

SPORTS

Vocabulary

<u>English word word</u>	<u>French</u>		
Team sport	**un sport collectif**	Handball	**le handball**
Individual sport	**un sport individuel**	Volleyball	**le volleyball**
Martial arts	**les arts martiaux**	Badminton	**le badminton**
The activities	**les activités**	Tennis	**le tennis**
Football	**le football**	Table tennis	**le tennis de table**
Basketball	**le basketball**	Swimming-pool	**la piscine**
		Ice hockey	**le hockey sur glace**

Rugby	**le rugby**	Cycling	**le cyclisme**
Water-polo	**le water-polo**	Horse riding	**l'équitation**
Baseball	**le baseball**	Figure skating	**le patinage**
Softball	**le softball**	Karate	**le karaté**
Cricket	**le cricket**	Skiing	**le ski**
English word	French word	Snowboard	**le snowboard**
Canoeing	**le canoé**	Shooting sport	**le tir sportif**
Athletics	**l'athlétisme**	Rowing	**l'aviron**
Boxing	**la boxe**	Sailing	**la voile**
Weightlifting	**l'haltérophilie**	Fencing	**l'escrime**
Judo	**le judo**	Gymnastics	**la gymnastique**
Wrestling	**la lutte**	Archery	**le tir à l'arc**

Dialogs

<u>Dialog 1</u>

What did you do this afternoon? **Qu'as-tu fait cet après-midi ?**

I went to the swimming pool. **Je suis allée à la piscine.**

<u>Dialog 2</u>

How often do you play table tennis? **À quelle fréquence joues-tu au tennis de table ?**

I play table tennis twice a week. **Je joue au tennis de table deux fois par semaine.**

<u>Dialog 3</u>

Does your sister play basketball with you? **Ta sœur joue-t-elle au basketball avec toi ?**

No, she'd rather go horse riding. **Non, elle préfère faire du cheval.**

<u>Dialog 4</u>

During holidays I always to go the beach. **Pendant les vacances, je vais toujours à la plage.**

That's great, do you like sailing? **C'est super, aimes-tu faire de la voile ?**

Practice

English :   swimming-pool

French :   **piscine**

Repeat :   **piscine**

Repeat :   **piscine**

Spell :   **p-i-s-c-i-n-e**

Spell :   **p-i-s-c-i-n-e**

In a phrase :   **Je suis allée à la piscine.**   *I went to the swimming-pool.*

Repeat :   **Je suis allée à la piscine.** *I went to the swimming-pool.*

Repeat :   **Je suis allée à la piscine.** *I went to the swimming-pool.*

Repeat :   **Je suis allée à la piscine.** *I went to the swimming-pool.*

English :   table tennis

French :   **tennis de table**

Repeat :   **tennis de table**

Repeat :   **tennis de table**

Spell :   **t-e-n-n-i-s-d-e-t-a-b-l-e**

Spell :   **t-e-n-n-i-s-d-e-t-a-b-l-e**

In a phrase : **Je joue au tennis de table deux fois par semaine**
I play table tennis twice a week.

Repeat :   **Je joue au tennis de table deux fois par semaine**
I play table tennis twice a week.

Repeat :   **Je joue au tennis de table deux fois par semaine**
I play table tennis twice a week.

Repeat :   **Je joue au tennis de table deux fois par semaine**
I play table tennis twice a week.

English :   go horse riding

French :   **faire du cheval**

Repeat :   **faire du cheval**

Repeat :   **faire du cheval**

Spell :   **f-a-i-r-e-d-u-c-h-e-v-a-l**

Spell :   **f-a-i-r-e-d-u-c-h-e-v-a-l**

In a phrase : **Non, elle préfère faire du cheval.**   *No, she'd rather go horse riding.*

Repeat :   **Non, elle préfère faire du cheval.**   *No, she'd rather go horse riding.*

Repeat :   **Non, elle préfère faire du cheval.** *No, she'd rather go horse riding.*

Repeat :   **Non, elle préfère faire du cheval.** *No, she'd rather go horse riding.*

English :   sailing

French :   **la voile**

Repeat :   **la voile**

Repeat :   **la voile**

Spell :   **l-a-v-o-i-l-e**

Spell :   **l-a-v-o-i-l-e**

In a phrase : **C'est super, aimes-tu faire de la voile ?** *That's great, do you like sailing?*

Repeat :   **C'est super, aimes-tu faire de la voile ?** *That's great, do you like sailing?*

Repeat :   **C'est super, aimes-tu faire de la voile ?** *That's great, do you like sailing?*

Repeat :   **C'est super, aimes-tu faire de la voile ?** *That's great, do you like sailing?*

MUSIC

Vocabulary

<u>English word word</u>	<u>French</u>
The accordion	**l'accordéon**
The alto	**l'alto**
The banjo	**le banjo**
The bass guitar	**la basse**
Drums	**la batterie**
The bugle	**le clairon**
Bagpipes	**la cornemuse**
The djembe	**le djembé**
The flute	**la flûte**
The guitar	**la guitare**

The harmonica	**l'harmonica**
The harp	**la harpe**

<u>English word word</u>	<u>French</u>
The mandolin	**la mandoline**
The metronome	**le métronome**
The organ	**l'orgue**
The piano	**le piano**
The saxophone	**le saxophone**
The whistle	**le sifflet**
Timpani	**les timbales**
The triangle	**le triangle**

The trumpet **la trompette**

The cello **le violoncelle**

The tuba **le tuba**

The violon **le violon**

Dialogs

Dialog 1

Do you play any music instrument? **Joues-tu d'un instrument de musique ?**

Yes, I play the piano. **Oui, je joue du piano.**

Dialog 2

Why does she go to the church so often? **Pourquoi va-t-elle à l'église si souvent ?**

She plays the organ there. **Elle y joue de l'orgue.**

Dialog 3

This man is very famous. **Cet homme est très connu.**

Yes, he plays the cello. **Oui, il joue du violoncelle.**

<u>Dialog 4</u>

John wants to start a new activity. **John veut commencer une nouvelle activité.**

He wants to play drums. **Il veut jouer de la batterie.**

Practice

English :   piano

French :   **piano**

Repeat :   **piano**

Repeat :   **piano**

Spell :   **p-i-a-n-o**

Spell :   **p-i-a-n-o**

In a phrase :   **Oui, je joue du piano.**   *Yes, I play the piano.*

Repeat :   **Oui, je joue du piano.**   *Yes, I play the piano.*

Repeat :   **Oui, je joue du piano.**   *Yes, I play the piano.*

Repeat :   **Oui, je joue du piano.**   *Yes, I play the piano.*

English :   organ

French :   **orgue**

Repeat :   **orgue**

Repeat :   **orgue**

Spell :   **o-r-g-u-e**

Spell :   **o-r-g-u-e**

In a phrase :   **Elle y joue de l'orgue.**   *She plays the organ there.*

Repeat :   **Elle y joue de l'orgue.**   *She plays the organ there.*

Repeat :   **Elle y joue de l'orgue.**   *She plays the organ there.*

Repeat :   **Elle y joue de l'orgue.**   *She plays the organ there.*

English :   cello

French :   **violoncelle**

Repeat :   **violoncelle**

Repeat :   **violoncelle**

Spell :   **v-i-o-l-o-n-c-e-l-l-e**

Spell :   **v-i-o-l-o-n-c-e-l-l-e**

In a phrase : **Oui, il joue du violoncelle.** *Yes, he plays the cello.*

Repeat : **Oui, il joue du violoncelle.** *Yes, he plays the cello.*

Repeat : **Oui, il joue du violoncelle.** *Yes, he plays the cello.*

Repeat : **Oui, il joue du violoncelle.** *Yes, he plays the cello.*

English : drums

French : **batterie**

Repeat : **batterie**

Repeat : **batterie**

Spell : **b-a-t-t-e-r-i-e**

Spell : **b-a-t-t-e-r-i-e**

In a phrase : **Il veut jouer de la batterie.** *He wants to plays drums.*

Repeat : **Il veut jouer de la batterie.** *He wants to plays drums.*

Repeat : **Il veut jouer de la batterie.** *He wants to plays drums.*

Repeat :   **Il veut jouer de la batterie.**   *He wants to plays drums.*

GAMES

Vocabulary

English word	French word	English word	French word
Outdoor games	**jeux d'extérieur**	Swing	**la balançoire**
Indoor games	**jeux d'intérieur**	Tobbogan	**tobbogan**
Marble game	**jeu de billes**	Treasure hunt	**chasse au trésor**
Dodgeball	**balle aux prisonniers**	Musical chairs	**les chaises musicales**
Hopscotch	**la marelle**	Sack race	**course de sac**
Pétanque	**la pétanque**	Statues	**1 2 3 soleil**
Bowling	**jeu de quilles**	Tug of war	**tir à la corde**

Coconut shy	**chamboule tout**	Puzzle	**casse-tête**
Tag game	**loup glacé**	Guessing game	**devinettes**
British bulldog	**l'épervier**	Gambling game	**jeu d'argent**
Leapfrog	**saute-mouton**	Game of mental skill	**jeu de réflexion**
Strategy game	**jeu de stratégie**	Card game	**jeu de cartes**
Game show	**jeu télévisé**	Board game	**jeu de société**
Jigsaw puzzle	**puzzle**	Video game	**jeu vidéo**

Dialogs

Dialog 1

Do you have a swing at home? **As-tu une balançoire à la maison ?**

Yes, in the garden. **Oui, dans le jardin.**

Dialog 2

Which board game would you like to play? **À quel jeu de société aimes-tu jouer ?**

I am fond of monopoly. **J'adore
le monopoly.**

<u>Dialog 3</u>

Peter is inventing new games. **Peter est
en train d'inventer de nouveaux jeux.**

He should play a guessing game. **Il devrait jouer
aux devinettes.**

<u>Dialog 4</u>

Peter and John are playing in the garden. **Peter et John
sont en train de jouer dans le jardin.**

They are playing leapfrog. **Ils sont en train
de jouer à saute-mouton.**

Practice

English :   swing

French :   **balançoire**

Repeat :   **balançoire**

Repeat :   **balançoire**

Spell :   **b-a-l-a-n-ç-o-i-r-e**

Spell :   **b-a-l-a-n-ç-o-i-r-e**

In a phrase : **As-tu une balançoire à la maison ?** *Do you have a swing at home?*

Repeat : **As-tu une balançoire à la maison ?** *Do you have a swing at home?*

Repeat : **As-tu une balançoire à la maison ?** *Do you have a swing at home?*

Repeat : **As-tu une balançoire à la maison ?** *Do you have a swing at home?*

English : board game

French : **jeu de société**

Repeat : **jeu de société**

Repeat : **jeu de société**

Spell : **j-e-u-d-e-s-o-c-i-é-t-é**

Spell : **j-e-u-d-e-s-o-c-i-é-t-é**

In a phrase : **À quel jeu de société aimes-tu jouer ?** *Which board game do you like to play?*

Repeat : **À quel jeu de société aimes-tu jouer ?** *Which board game do you like to play?*

Repeat : **À quel jeu de société aimes-tu jouer ?** *Which board game do you like to play?*

Repeat :   **À quel jeu de société aimes-tu jouer ?**   ***Which board game do you like to play?***

English :   guessing game

French :   **devinettes**

Repeat :   **devinettes**

Repeat :   **devinettes**

Spell :   **d-e-v-i-n-e-t-t-e-s**

Spell :   **d-e-v-i-n-e-t-t-e-s**

In a phrase :   **Il devrait jouer aux devinettes.**   ***He should play a guessing game.***

Repeat :   **Il devrait jouer aux devinettes.**   ***He should play a guessing game.***

Repeat :   **Il devrait jouer aux devinettes.**   ***He should play a guessing game.***

Repeat :   **Il devrait jouer aux devinettes.**   ***He should play a guessing game.***

English :   leapfrog

French :   **saute-mouton**

Repeat :   **saute-mouton**

Repeat :   **saute-mouton**

Spell :   **s-a-u-t-e-m-o-u-t-o-n**

Spell :   **s-a-u-t-e-m-o-u-t-o-n**

In a phrase :   **Ils sont en train de jouer à saute-mouton.** *They are playing leapfrog.*

Repeat :   **Ils sont en train de jouer à saute-mouton.** *They are playing leapfrog.*

Repeat :   **Ils sont en train de jouer à saute-mouton.** *They are playing leapfrog.*

Repeat :   **Ils sont en train de jouer à saute-mouton.** *They are playing leapfrog.*

Chapter 5: AT HOME

You spend a lot of time at home as well. It is important to use the accurate vocabulary when talking about it. Let's talk about it in French!

MY HOUSE

Vocabulary

English word	French word
The house, home	**la maison**
The flat, apartment	**l'appartement**
The hall	**le hall**
The living-room	**la salle à manger**
The bedroom	**la chambre**
The basement	**le sous-sol**
The cellar	**la cave**
The attic	**le grenier**
The ground-floor	**le rez-de-chaussée**
The first floor	**le premier étage**
The stairs	**l'escalier**
The elevator	**l'ascenseur**
The door	**la porte**
The window	**la fenêtre**

The wall	**le mur**
The ceiling	**le plafond**
The chandelier	**le lustre**
The kitchen	**la cuisine**
The table	**la table**
The chair	**la chaise**
The fridge	**le réfrigérateur**
The micro-wave	**le micro-onde**

<u>English word</u>	<u>French word</u>
The oven	**le four**
The toaster	**le grille-pain**
The sink	**l'évier**
The dishwasher	**le lave-vaisselle**
The plate	**l'assiette**
The glass	**le verre**
The fork	**la fourchette**
The knife	**le couteau**
The cup	**la tasse**
The bottle	**la bouteille**
The napkin	**la serviette**
The tablecloth	**la nappe**
The apron	**le tablier**
The timer	**le minuteur**
The living-room	**le salon**
The couch, sofa	**le canapé**

English word	French
The armchair	le fauteuil
The coffee table	la table-basse
The television, TV	la télévision
The curtain	le rideau
The amp	l'ampli
The remote control	la télécommande

English word	French
The bookshelf	la bibliothèque
The bathroom	la salle de bain
The bath	la baignoire
The shower	la douche
The towel	la serviette

English word	French
The make-up	le maquillage
The shampoo	le shampoing
The soap	le savon
The shower gel	le gel douche
The toothpaste	le dentifrice
The toothbrush	la brosse à dents

English word	French
The medecine cabinet	l'armoire à pharmacie
The bedroom	la chambre
The bed	le lit
The bedside table	la table de chevet

The lamp   **la lampe**

The wardrobe   **l'armoire**

The cushion   **le coussin**

The pillow   **l'oreiller**

The duvet, quilt   **la couette**

The sheet   **le drap**

The office   **le bureau**

The desk   **le bureau**

Dialogs

Dialog 1

Where is your house?   **Où est ta maison?**

There, with the red gate.   **Là, avec le portail rouge.**

Dialog 2

Where is John?   **Où est John?**

John is in the kitchen.   **John est dans la cuisine.**

Dialog 3

Where is the document?   **Où est le document ?**

It is on the desk.   **Il est sur le bureau.**

Dialog 4

There is no elevator here. **Il n'y a pas
d'ascenseur ici.**

Yes, you need to climb up the stairs. **Oui, vous devez
monter les escaliers.**

Practice

English :   house

French :   **maison**

Repeat :   **maison**

Repeat :   **maison**

Spell :   **m-a-i-s-o-n**

Spell :   **m-a-i-s-o-n**

In a phrase : **Où est ta maison?** *Where is the house ?*

Repeat :   **Où est ta maison?** *Where is the house ?*

Repeat :   **Où est ta maison?** *Where is the house ?*

Repeat :   **Où est ta maison?** *Where is the house ?*

English :   kitchen

French :   **cuisine**

Repeat :   **cuisine**

Repeat :   **cuisine**

Spell :   **c-u-i-s-i-n-e**

Spell :   **c-u-i-s-i-n-e**

In a phrase :   **John est dans la cuisine.** *John is in the kitchen.*

Repeat :   **John est dans la cuisine.** *John is in the kitchen.*

Repeat :   **John est dans la cuisine.** *John is in the kitchen.*

Repeat :   **John est dans la cuisine.** *John is in the kitchen.*

English :   desk

French :   **bureau**

Repeat :   **bureau**

Repeat :   **bureau**

Spell :   **b-u-r-e-a-u**

Spell :   **b-u-r-e-a-u**

In a phrase :   **Il est sur le bureau.** *It is on the desk.*

Repeat :   **Il est sur le bureau.** *It is on the desk.*

Repeat :   **Il est sur le bureau.** *It is on the desk.*

Repeat :   **Il est sur le bureau.** *It is on the desk.*

English :   stairs

French :   **escaliers**

Repeat :   **escaliers**

Repeat :   **escaliers**

Spell :   **e-s-c-a-l-i-e-r-s**

Spell :   **e-s-c-a-l-i-e-r-s**

In a phrase :   **Oui, vous devez monter les escaliers. *Yes, you need to climb up the stairs.***

Repeat :   **Oui, vous devez monter les escaliers. *Yes, you need to climb up the stairs.***

Repeat :   **Oui, vous devez monter les escaliers. *Yes, you need to climb up the stairs.***

Repeat :   **Oui, vous devez monter les escaliers. *Yes, you need to climb up the stairs.***

OUTSIDE

Vocabulary

<u>English word</u>	<u>French</u>		
<u>word</u>		The gate, doorway	**le portail**

The garage	**le garage**
The garden	**le jardin**
The vegetable garden	**le potager**
The greenhouse	**la serre**
The rake	**le râteau**
The watering can	**l'arrosoir**
The car	**la voiture**
The trailer	**la remorque**
The mower	**la tondeuse**
The district	**le quartier**
The farm	**la ferme**
The cottage	**le chalet**

| The mobil-home | **le mobile-home** |

<u>English word</u>	<u>French word</u>
The villa	**la villa**
The mansion	**le manoir**
The castle	**le château**
The residency	**la résidence**
The building, block	**l'immeuble**
The farm	**la ferme**
The barn	**la grange**
The workbench	**l'établi**
The chicken coop	**le poulailler**
The field	**le champ**

| The tractor | **le tracteur** | The barn | **l'étable** |
| The pitchfork | **la fourche** | The hangar | **le hangar** |

Dialogs

<u>Dialog 1</u>

It's very sunny today. **Il fait très beau aujourd'hui.**

You can go to the garden. **Tu peux aller dans le jardin.**

<u>Dialog 2</u>

Do you live in New York? **Vis-tu à New-York ?**

Yes, in a quiet district. **Oui, dans un quartier calme.**

<u>Dialog 3</u>

France has lots of famous castles. **La France a beaucoup de châteaux connus.**

Yes, you can see them in the region called Loire. **Oui, tu peux les voir dans la région appelée la Loire.**

<u>Dialog 4</u>

Where does John come from? **D'où vient John ?**

He grew up in a farm. **Il a grandi à la ferme.**

Practice

English :   garden

French :   **jardin**

Repeat :   **jardin**

Repeat :   **jardin**

Spell :   **j-a-r-d-i-n**

Spell :   **j-a-r-d-i-n**

In a phrase :   **Tu peux aller dans le jardin.** *You can go to the garden.*

Repeat :   **Tu peux aller dans le jardin.** *You can go to the garden.*

Repeat :   **Tu peux aller dans le jardin.** *You can go to the garden.*

Repeat :   **Tu peux aller dans le jardin.** *You can go to the garden.*

English :   district

French :   **quartier**

Repeat :   **quartier**

Repeat :   **quartier**

Spell :   **q-u-a-r-t-i-e-r**

Spell :   **q-u-a-r-t-i-e-r**

In a phrase :   **Oui, dans un quartier calme.**   *Yes, in a quiet district.*

Repeat :   **Oui, dans un quartier calme.**   *Yes, in a quiet district.*

Repeat :   **Oui, dans un quartier calme.**   *Yes, in a quiet district.*

Repeat :   **Oui, dans un quartier calme.**   *Yes, in a quiet district.*

English :   castle

French :   **château**

Repeat :   **château**

Repeat :   **château**

Spell :   **c-h-â-t-e-a-u**

Spell :   **c-h-â-t-e-a-u**

In a phrase : **La France a beaucoup de châteaux connus.**
France has lots of famous castles.

Repeat : **La France a beaucoup de châteaux connus.**
France has lots of famous castles.

Repeat : **La France a beaucoup de châteaux connus.**
France has lots of famous castles.

Repeat : **La France a beaucoup de châteaux connus.**
France has lots of famous castles.

English : farm

French : **ferme**

Repeat : **ferme**

Repeat : **ferme**

Spell : **f-e-r-m-e**

Spell : **f-e-r-m-e**

In a phrase : **Il a grandi à la ferme.** *He grew up in a farm.*

Repeat : **Il a grandi à la ferme.** *He grew up in a farm.*

Repeat : **Il a grandi à la ferme.** *He grew up in a farm.*

Repeat : **Il a grandi à la ferme.** *He grew up in a farm.*

Chapter 6: AT SCHOOL

In this chapter, you'll learn all the usual words used at school. That's perfect if you want to talk about your everyday routine at school in French. The topics are the followings: places at school, in the classroom, levels and subjects

AT SCHOOL

Vocabulary

English word word	French		
Preschool	**la crèche**	Higher education	**l'enseignement supérieur**
Kindergarten	**la maternelle**	The building	**le bâtiment**
Primary school	**l'école primaire**	The classroom	**la salle de classe**
Middle school	**le collège**	The playground	**le préau**
Highschool	**le lycée**	The canteen	**la cantine**
The University	**l'université**	The library	**la bibliothèque**

The gymnasium **le gymnase**

The laboratory **le laboratoire**

The book **le livre**

The copybook **le manuel**

The pencilcase **la trousse**

The glue **la colle**

The ruler **le règle**

Scissors **les ciseaux**

The rubber **la gomme**

The desk **le bureau**

The blackboard **le tableau**

English word / French word

The schoolbag **le cartable**

The pen **le stylo**

The highlighter **le surligneur**

The workbook **le cahier d'activité**

The map **la carte**

The flag **le drapeau**

The computer **l'ordinateur**

The laptop **le portable**

The dictionary **le dictionnaire**

Sit down **Asseyez-vous**

Take your book **Prenez votre livre**

Open your book **Ouvrez votre livre**

Stand up **Levez-vous**

Raise your hand **Levez la main**

Listen to the teacher **Ecoutez le professeur**

Read the text **Lisez le texte**

Stay calm **Soyez calme**

Come into the class **Venez en classe**

Close your bag **Fermez votre sac**

The timetable **l'emploi du temps**

A mark **une note**

The rating **l'évaluation**

Dialogs

<u>Dialog 1</u>

The lesson has already started! **Le cours a déjà commencé !**

Come into the classroom! **Entrez dans la salle !**

<u>Dialog 2</u>

You live in a nice town! **Tu vis dans une ville sympa !**

Yes, here is our middle school. **Oui, et voici notre collège.**

<u>Dialog 3</u>

Can you give me your pen? **Peux-tu me donner ton stylo ?**

I can't find my pencil case.   **Je ne trouve pas ma trousse.**

Dialog 4

John, please come here.   **John, vient ici s'il te plait.**

Should I write the answer on the blackboard?   **Dois-je écrire la réponse au tableau ?**

Practice

English :   classroom

French :   **salle de classe**

Repeat :   **salle de classe**

Repeat :   **salle de classe**

Spell :   **s-a-l-l-e-d-e-c-l-a-s-s-e**

Spell :   **s-a-l-l-e-d-e-c-l-a-s-s-e**

In a phrase :   **Entrez dans la salle !** *Come into the classroom!*

Repeat :   **Entrez dans la salle !** *Come into the classroom!*

Repeat :   **Entrez dans la salle !** *Come into the classroom!*

Repeat :   **Entrez dans la salle !** *Come into the classroom!*

English :   middle school

French :   **collège**

Repeat :   **collège**

Repeat :   **collège**

Spell :   **c-o-l-l-è-g-e**

Spell :   **c-o-l-l-è-g-e**

In a phrase :   **Oui, et voici notre collège.**   *Yes, and here is our middle school.*

Repeat :   **Oui, et voici notre collège.**   *Yes, and here is our middle school.*

Repeat :   **Oui, et voici notre collège.**   *Yes, and here is our middle school.*

Repeat :   **Oui, et voici notre collège.**   *Yes, and here is our middle school.*

English :   pencil case

French :   **trousse**

Repeat :   **trousse**

Repeat :   **trousse**

Spell :   **t-r-o-u-s-s-e**

Spell :   **t-r-o-u-s-s-e**

In a phrase : **Je ne trouve pas ma trousse.** *I can't find my pencil case.*

Repeat : **Je ne trouve pas ma trousse.** *I can't find my pencil case.*

Repeat : **Je ne trouve pas ma trousse.** *I can't find my pencil case.*

Repeat : **Je ne trouve pas ma trousse.** *I can't find my pencil case.*

English : blackboard

French : **tableau**

Repeat : **tableau**

Repeat : **tableau**

Spell : **t-a-b-l-e-a-u**

Spell : **t-a-b-l-e-a-u**

In a phrase : **Dois-je écrire la réponse au tableau ?** *Should I write the answer on the board?*

Repeat : **Dois-je écrire la réponse au tableau ?** *Should I write the answer on the board?*

Repeat : **Dois-je écrire la réponse au tableau ?** *Should I write the answer on the board?*

Repeat :   **Dois-je écrire la réponse au tableau ?**   *Should I write the answer on the board?*

LEVELS & SUBJECTS

Vocabulary

English word	French word
A subject	**une matière**
English	**anglais**
French	**français**
Spanish	**espagnol**
German	**allemand**
Maths	**maths**
History	**histoire**
Geography	**géographie**
Technology	**technologie**
IT	**informatique**
PE	**sport**
RE	**catéchisme**

English word	French word
Science	**les sciences**
Mordern languages	**LVE**
Music	**musique**
The break	**la pause**

Studies
des études

6th grade **sixième**

7th grade
cinquième

8th grade
quatrième

9th grade
troisième

10th grade
seconde

11th grade
première

12th grade
terminale

Dialogs

Dialog 1

You're new at school! **Tu es nouveau à l'école !**

Yes, I'm in the 6th grade. **Oui, je suis en sixième.**

Dialog2

What is your favourite subject? **Quelle est ta matière préférée ?**

I love French! **J'adore le français !**

Dialog 3

P.E was my best subject! **Le sport était ma matière préférée !**

That is not surprising! **Ce n'est pas surprenant !**

<u>Dialog 4</u>

I didn't like I.T at school. **Je n'aimais pas l'informatique à l'école.**

That's not possible, you're a geek! **Ce n'est pas possible, tu es un geek !**

Practice

English :	6th grade

French :	**sixième**

Repeat :	**sixième**

Repeat :	**sixième**

Spell :	**s-i-x-i-è-m-e**

Spell :	**s-i-x-i-è-m-e**

In a phrase :	**Oui, je suis en sixième.** *Yes, I'm in the 6th grade.*

Repeat :	**Oui, je suis en sixième.** *Yes, I'm in the 6th grade.*

Repeat :	**Oui, je suis en sixième.** *Yes, I'm in the 6th grade.*

Repeat :	**Oui, je suis en sixième.** *Yes, I'm in the 6th grade.*

English :   subject

French :   **matière**

Repeat :   **matière**

Repeat :   **matière**

Spell :   **m-a-t-i-è-r-e**

Spell :   **m-a-t-i-è-r-e**

In a phrase : **Quelle est ta matière préférée ?** *What is your favourite subject?*

Repeat :   **Quelle est ta matière préférée ?** *What is your favourite subject?*

Repeat :   **Quelle est ta matière préférée ?** *What is your favourite subject?*

Repeat :   **Quelle est ta matière préférée ?** *What is your favourite subject?*

English :   P.E.

French :   **sport**

Repeat :   **sport**

Repeat :   **sport**

Spell :   **s-p-o-r-t**

Spell :   **s-p-o-r-t**

In a phrase : **Le sport était ma matière préférée !** *P.E was my best subject!*

Repeat : **Le sport était ma matière préférée !** *P.E was my best subject!*

Repeat : **Le sport était ma matière préférée !** *P.E was my best subject!*

Repeat : **Le sport était ma matière préférée !** *P.E was my best subject!*

English : I.T.

French : **informatique**

Repeat : **informatique**

Repeat : **informatique**

Spell : **i-n-f-o-r-m-a-t-i-q-u-e**

Spell : **i-n-f-o-r-m-a-t-i-q-u-e**

In a phrase : **Je n'aimais pas l'informatique à l'école.** *I didn't like I.T at school.*

Repeat : **Je n'aimais pas l'informatique à l'école.** *I didn't like I.T at school.*

Repeat : **Je n'aimais pas l'informatique à l'école.** *I didn't like I.T at school.*

Repeat : **Je n'aimais pas l'informatique à l'école.** *I didn't like I.T at school.*

Chapter 7: FOOD

Talking about your routine implies that you talk about what you like in your everyday life and what you eat! You will be able to say what you eat during breakfast, at lunch or for dinner. Let's review the key words in French!

FRUITS

Vocabulary

English word word	French
Apple	**pomme**
Apricot	**abricot**
Plum	**prune**
Grape	**raisin**
Banana	**banane**
Cherry	**cerise**
Lemon	**citron**

Orange	**orange**
Pear	**poire**
Peach	**pèche**
Pineapple	**ananas**
Strawberry	**fraise**
Raspberry	**framboise**
Blackberry	**mûre**
Blueberry	**myrtille**

English word	French word
Passion fruit	**fruit de la passion**
Pomegranate	**grenade**
Blackcurrant	**cassis**
Redcurrant	**groseille**
Kiwi	**kiwi**
Cranberries	**airelles**
Almond	**amande**
Chestnut	**châtaigne**
Clementine	**clémentine**
Quince	**coing**
Walnut	**noix**
Fig	**figue**
Lychee	**litchi**
Mango	**mangue**
Melon	**melon**
Watermelon	**pastèque**
Grapefruit	**pamplemousse**

Dialogs

Dialog 1

What are you eating?   **Que manges-tu?**

I'm eating cherries.   **Je mange des cerises.**

Dialog 2

What have you bought? **Qu'as-tu acheté ?**

I've bought grapes. **J'ai acheté du raisin.**

Dialog 3

You need to eat fruit as well. **Tu dois manger des fruits aussi.**

I've eaten an apple. **J'ai mangé une pomme.**

Dialog 4

Which fruit is your favourite? **Quel fruit est ton préféré ?**

I really like strawberries. **J'aime vraiment les fraises.**

Practice

English :   cherry

French :   **cerise**

Repeat :   **cerise**

Repeat :   **cerise**

Spell :   **c-e-r-i-s-e**

Spell :   **c-e-r-i-s-e**

In a phrase :   **Je mange des cerises.** *I'm eating cherries.*

Repeat :   **Je mange des cerises.** *I'm eating cherries.*

Repeat :   **Je mange des cerises.** *I'm eating cherries.*

Repeat :   **Je mange des cerises.** *I'm eating cherries.*

English :   grape

French :   **raisin**

Repeat :   **raisin**

Repeat :   **raisin**

Spell :   **r-a-i-s-i-n**

Spell :   **r-a-i-s-i-n**

In a phrase :   **J'ai acheté du raisin.** *I've bought grapes.*

Repeat :   **J'ai acheté du raisin.** *I've bought grapes.*

Repeat :   **J'ai acheté du raisin.** *I've bought grapes.*

Repeat :   **J'ai acheté du raisin.** *I've bought grapes.*

English :   apple

French :   **pomme**

Repeat :   **pomme**

Repeat :   **pomme**

Spell :   **p-o-m-m-e**

Spell :   **p-o-m-m-e**

In a phrase : **J'ai mangé une pomme.** *I've eaten an apple.*

Repeat :   **J'ai mangé une pomme.** *I've eaten an apple.*

Repeat :   **J'ai mangé une pomme.** *I've eaten an apple.*

Repeat :   **J'ai mangé une pomme.** *I've eaten an apple.*

English :   strawberry

French :   **fraise**

Repeat :   **fraise**

Repeat :   **fraise**

Spell :   **f-r-a-i-s-e**

Spell :   **f-r-a-i-s-e**

In a phrase : **J'aime vraiment les fraises.**   *I really like strawberries.*

Repeat :   **J'aime vraiment les fraises.**   *I really like strawberries.*

Repeat :   **J'aime vraiment les fraises.**   *I really like strawberries.*

Repeat :   **J'aime vraiment les fraises.**   *I really like strawberries.*

VEGETABLES

Vocabulary

English word word	French
Artichoke	**artichaut**

English word word	French
Avocado	**avocat**
Beetroot	**betterave**
Broccoli	**brocoli**
Mushroom	**champignon**
Pickle	**cornichon**

Baked bean	**flageolet**
Ginger	**gingembre**
Yam	**igname**
Lentil	**lentille**
Olive	**olive**
Rhubarb	**rhubarbe**
Rutabaga	**rutabaga**
Soya	**soja**
Fennel	**fenouil**
Corn	**maïs**

Turnip	**navet**	Eggplant	**aubergine**
Pepper	**poivron**	Butternut	**courge musquée**
Cabbage	**chou**	Pumpkin	**citrouille**
Carrot	**carotte**	Cauliflower	**chou-fleur**
Peas	**pois**	Brussels sprout	**chou de bruxelles**
Potato	**patate**	Kale	**chou frisé**
Spinach	**épinard**	Celery	**céleri**
Tomato	**tomate**	Leek	**poireau**
Cucumber	**concombre**	Salsify	**salsifi**
Zucchini	**courgette**		

Dialogs

<u>Dialog 1</u>

What are you going to eat with the meat? **Que vas-tu manger avec la viande ?**

I've ordered some green peas. **J'ai commandé des petits pois.**

<u>Dialog 2</u>

It's easy to get some tomatoes.   **C'est facile d'obtenir des tomates.**

Yes, it's the summer.   **Oui, c'est l'été.**

<u>Dialog 3</u>

What have you cooked for dinner?   **Qu'as-tu cuisiné pour le dîner ?**

I've baked some potatoes.   **J'ai cuit au four des patates.**

<u>Dialog 4</u>

Dinner is ready!   **Le dîner est prêt !**

Great, you added mushrooms!   **Super, tu as ajouté des champignons !**

Practice

English :   green peas

French :   **petits pois**

Repeat :   **petits pois**

Repeat :   **petits pois**

Spell :   **p-e-t-i-t-s-p-o-i-s**

Spell :   **p-e-t-i-t-s-p-o-i-s**

In a phrase :   **J'ai commandé des petits pois.**   *I've ordered some green peas.*

Repeat :   **J'ai commandé des petits pois.**   *I've ordered some green peas.*

Repeat :   **J'ai commandé des petits pois.**   *I've ordered some green peas.*

Repeat :   **J'ai commandé des petits pois.**   *I've ordered some green peas.*

English :   tomato

French :   **tomate**

Repeat :   **tomate**

Repeat :   **tomate**

Spell :   **t-o-m-a-t-e**

Spell :   **t-o-m-a-t-e**

In a phrase :   **C'est facile d'obtenir des tomates.**   *It's easy to get some tomatoes.*

Repeat :   **C'est facile d'obtenir des tomates.**   *It's easy to get some tomatoes.*

Repeat :   **C'est facile d'obtenir des tomates.**   *It's easy to get some tomatoes.*

Repeat :	**C'est facile d'obtenir des tomates.** *It's easy to get some tomatoes.*

English :	ptotato

French :	**patate**

Repeat :	**patate**

Repeat :	**patate**

Spell :	**p-a-t-a-t-e**

Spell :	**p-a-t-a-t-e**

In a phrase :	**J'ai cuit au four des patates.** *I've baked some potatoes.*

Repeat :	**J'ai cuit au four des patates.** *I've baked some potatoes.*

Repeat :	**J'ai cuit au four des patates.** *I've baked some potatoes.*

Repeat :	**J'ai cuit au four des patates.** *I've baked some potatoes.*

English :	mushroom

French :	**champignon**

Repeat :	**champignon**

Repeat :   **champignon**

Spell :   **c-h-a-m-p-i-g-n-o-n**

Spell :   **c-h-a-m-p-i-g-n-o-n**

In a phrase : **Super, tu as ajouté des champignons !** *Great, you added mushooms!*

Repeat :   **Super, tu as ajouté des champignons !** *Great, you added mushooms!*

Repeat :   **Super, tu as ajouté des champignons !** *Great, you added mushooms!*

Repeat :   **Super, tu as ajouté des champignons !** *Great, you added mushooms!*

MEAT AND FISH

Vocabulary

English word	French		
Meat	**viande**	Roast beef	**roast beef**
Ham	**jambon**	Pork loin	**longe de porc**
Beef	**boeuf**	Bacon	**bacon**
		Lamb ribs	**côte d'agneau**

English word	French word
Chicken roast	**poulet rôti**
Chicken legs	**cuisses de poulet**
Chicken breast	**poitrine de poulet**

English word	French word
Chicken wings	**ailes de Poulet**
Grilled chicken	**poulet grille**
Turkey	**dinde**
Duck	**canard**
Meat balls	**boulettes**
Sausage	**saussice**
Seafood	**fruit de mer**
Trout	**truite**
Salmon	**saumon**
Tuna	**ton**

English word	French word
Cod	**cabillaud**
Snapper	**vivaneau**
Maquerel	**maquereau**
Crab	**crabe**
Eel	**anguille**
Abalone	**Ormeau**

English word	French word
Clams	**palourde**
Oysters	**huitres**
Lobster	**homard**

Mussel   **moule**   Cockles

Shrimp   **coque**

     crevette   Octopus   **pieuvre**

Dialogs

Dialog 1

Do you like meat?   **Aimes-tu la viande ?**

No, I am a vegetarian.   **Non, je suis végétarien.**

Dialog 2

Muslims can't eat ham.   **Les musulmans ne peuvent pas manger de jambon.**

Yes, it is forbidden by the religion.   **Oui, c'est interdit par la religion.**

Dialog 3

What do Americans eat for Thanksgiving?   **Que mangent les américains pour Thanksgiving ?**

They eat turkey.   **Ils mangent de la dinde.**

Dialog 4

Some people hate fish.   **Certaines personnes détestent le poisson.**

But salmon has essential nutrients.   **Mais le saumon contient des nutriments essentiels.**

Practice

English :   meat

French :   **viande**

Repeat :   **viande**

Repeat :   **viande**

Spell :   **v-i-a-n-d-e**

Spell :   **v-i-a-n-d-e**

In a phrase : **Aimes-tu la viande ?** *Do you like meat?*

Repeat :   **Aimes-tu la viande ?** *Do you like meat?*

Repeat :   **Aimes-tu la viande ?** *Do you like meat?*

Repeat :   **Aimes-tu la viande ?** *Do you like meat?*

English :   ham

French :   **jambon**

Repeat :   **jambon**

Repeat :   **jambon**

Spell :   **j-a-m-b-o-n**

Spell :   **j-a-m-b-o-n**

In a phrase :   **Les musulmans ne peuvent pas manger de jambon.** *Muslims can't eat ham.*

Repeat :   **Les musulmans ne peuvent pas manger de jambon.** *Muslims can't eat ham.*

Repeat :   **Les musulmans ne peuvent pas manger de jambon.** *Muslims can't eat ham.*

Repeat :   **Les musulmans ne peuvent pas manger de jambon.** *Muslims can't eat ham.*

English :   turkey

French :   **dinde**

Repeat :   **dinde**

Repeat :   **dinde**

Spell :   **d-i-n-d-e**

Spell :   **d-i-n-d-e**

In a phrase :   **Ils mangent de la dinde.** *They eat turkey.*

Repeat :   **Ils mangent de la dinde.** *They eat turkey.*

Repeat :   **Ils mangent de la dinde.** *They eat turkey.*

Repeat :   **Ils mangent de la dinde.** *They eat turkey.*

English :   salmon

French :   **saumon**

Repeat :   **saumon**

Repeat :   **saumon**

Spell :   **s-a-u-m-o-n**

Spell :   **s-a-u-m-o-n**

In a phrase : **Mais le saumon contient des nutriments essentiels.** *But the salmon has essential nutrients.*

Repeat : **Mais le saumon contient des nutriments essentiels.** *But the salmon has essential nutrients.*

Repeat : **Mais le saumon contient des nutriments essentiels.** *But the salmon has essential nutrients.*

Repeat : **Mais le saumon contient des nutriments essentiels.** *But the salmon has essential nutrients.*

DAIRY PRODUCTS, OTHER FOOD AND TASTE

Vocabulary

English word word	French	Dairy products
		les produits laitiers
	Milk	**le lait**

Butter	le crème
Cream	la crème
Yoghurt	le yaourt
Cheese	le fromage
Egg	oeuf
Salt	du sel
Pepper	du poivre
French fries, chips	frites
Crisps	chips
Pasta	pates
Rice	riz
Salad	salade
Rocket	roquette
Lettuce	laitue

English word	French
Endive	endive
Cress	cresson
Corn salad	mâche
Cake	gâteau
Chocolate	chocolat
Vanilla	vanille
Cookies	cookie
Coffee	café
Garlic	ail
Onion	oignon
Shallot	échalote
Tea	thé
Tasty	bon
I like	J'aime bien
I love	J'adore

| I hate | **Je déteste** | I'm crazy about | **Je suis fou de** |

Dialogs

Dialog 1

Some people don't like cheese. **Certaines personnes n'aiment pas le fromage.**

Cheese is good for the bones. **Le fromage est bon pour les os.**

Dialog 2

What is the food teenagers like? **Quelle nourriture les adolescents aiment-ils ?**

All teenagers like French fries. **Tous les adolescents aiment les frites.**

Dialog 3

The menu contains fish. **Le menu contient du poisson.**

Fish is served on Fridays. **Le poisson est servi les vendredis.**

Dialog 4

What is your favourite meal for breakfast? **Quel est votre plat préféré pour le petit-déjeuner ?**

I'm crazy about crambled eggs.   **J'adore
les oeufs brouillés.**

Practice

English :   cheese

French :   **fromage**

Repeat :   **fromage**

Repeat :   **fromage**

Spell :   **f-r-o-m-a-g-e**

Spell :   **f-r-o-m-a-g-e**

In a phrase : **Le fromage est bon pour les os.** *Cheese is good for the bones.*

Repeat :   **Le fromage est bon pour les os.** *Cheese is good for the bones.*

Repeat :   **Le fromage est bon pour les os.** *Cheese is good for the bones.*

Repeat :   **Le fromage est bon pour les os.** *Cheese is good for the bones.*

English :   french fries

French :   **frites**

Repeat :   **frites**

Repeat :   **frites**

Spell :   **f-r-i-t-e-s**

Spell :   **f-r-i-t-e-s**

In a phrase :   **Tous les adolescents aiment les frites.**   *All teenagers like French fries.*

Repeat :   **Tous les adolescents aiment les frites.**   *All teenagers like French fries.*

Repeat :   **Tous les adolescents aiment les frites.**   *All teenagers like French fries.*

Repeat :   **Tous les adolescents aiment les frites.**   *All teenagers like French fries.*

English :   fish

French :   **poisson**

Repeat :   **poisson**

Repeat :   **poisson**

Spell :   **p-o-i-s-s-o-n**

Spell :   **p-o-i-s-s-o-n**

In a phrase :   **Le poisson est servi les vendredis.**   *Fish is served on Fridays.*

Repeat :   **Le poisson est servi les vendredis.**   *Fish is served on Fridays.*

Repeat :   **Le poisson est servi les vendredis.**   *Fish is served on Fridays.*

Repeat :   **Le poisson est servi les vendredis.**   *Fish is served on Fridays.*

English :   egg

French :   **oeuf**

Repeat :   **oeuf**

Repeat :   **oeuf**

Spell :   **o-e-u-f**

Spell :   **o-e-u-f**

In a phrase :   **J'adore les oeufs brouillés.**   *I love crambled eggs.*

Repeat :   **J'adore les oeufs brouillés.**   *I love crambled eggs.*

Repeat :   **J'adore les oeufs brouillés.**   *I love crambled eggs.*

Repeat :   **J'adore les oeufs brouillés.**   *I love crambled eggs.*

Chapter 8: IN TOWN

We always need to go to the town in our everyday life. It is therefore important to know how you can talk about your routine in town in French. Here is a useful list.

GOING TO TOWN

Vocabulary

English word word	French	English word word	French
A car	**une voiture**	A van	**une fourgonnette**
A station wagon	**un break**	A company car	**une voiture de fonction**
A scooter	**un scooter**	To drive a car	**conduire une voiture**
A kick scooter	**une trottinette**	To ride a bike	**rouler à vélo**
A trailer	**une remorque**	To walk	**marcher**
A lorry, truck	**un camion**		

To run **courir**

To park **se garer**

To go **aller**

To go back **revenir, rentrer**

To turn left **tourner à gauche**

To turn right **tourner à droite**

To go straight away **aller tout droit**

To cross **traverser**

To stop **s'arrêter**

Dialogs

<u>Dialog 1</u>

I need to go to this shop. **Je dois aller dans ce magasin.**

Park your car here. **Gare ta voiture ici.**

<u>Dialog 2</u>

How do you go to school? **Comment vas-tu à l'école ?**

I ride a bike everyday. **J'y vais en vélo tous les jours.**

<u>Dialog 3</u>

Are you tired? **Es-tu fatigué?**

No, we can walk up the street.   **Non,
nous pouvons remonter la rue en marchant.**

<u>Dialog 4</u>

Do you need to go shopping?   **As-tu besoin de
faire les magasins ?**

No, we can go back home.   **Nous,   nous
pouvons rentrer à la maison.**

Practice

English :   car

French :   **voiture**

Repeat :   **voiture**

Repeat :   **voiture**

Spell :   **v-o-i-t-u-r-e**

Spell :   **v-o-i-t-u-r-e**

In a phrase :   **Gare ta voiture ici.** *Park your car here.*

Repeat :   **Gare ta voiture ici.** *Park your car here.*

Repeat :   **Gare ta voiture ici.** *Park your car here.*

Repeat :   **Gare ta voiture ici.** *Park your car here.*

English :   bike

French :   **vélo**

Repeat :   **vélo**

Repeat :   **vélo**

Spell :   **v-é-l-o**

Spell :   **v-é-l-o**

In a phrase :   **J'y vais en vélo tous les jours.**   *L ride a bike everyday.*

Repeat :   **J'y vais en vélo tous les jours.**   *L ride a bike everyday.*

Repeat :   **J'y vais en vélo tous les jours.**   *L ride a bike everyday.*

Repeat :   **J'y vais en vélo tous les jours.**   *L ride a bike everyday.*

English :   walk

French :   **marcher**

Repeat :   **marcher**

Repeat :   **marcher**

Spell :   **m-a-r-c-h-e-r**

Spell :   **m-a-r-c-h-e-r**

In a phrase : **J'adore les oeufs brouillés.** *I love crambled eggs.*

Repeat : **J'adore les oeufs brouillés.** *I love crambled eggs.*

Repeat : **J'adore les oeufs brouillés.** *I love crambled eggs.*

Repeat : **J'adore les oeufs brouillés.** *I love crambled eggs.*

English : go back

French : **rentrer**

Repeat : **rentrer**

Repeat : **rentrer**

Spell : **r-e-n-t-r-e-r**

Spell : **r-e-n-t-r-e-r**

In a phrase : **Nous, nous pouvons rentrer à la maison.** *No, we can go back home.*

Repeat : **Nous, nous pouvons rentrer à la maison.** *No, we can go back home.*

Repeat : **Nous, nous pouvons rentrer à la maison.** *No, we can go back home.*

Repeat :   **Nous, nous pouvons rentrer à la maison.**   *No, we can go back home.*

PLACES IN TOWN

Vocabulary

English word word	French
The city	**la ville**
The countryside	**la campagne**
The township	**la commune**
The street	**la rue**
The road	**la route**
The way	**la voie**
The cycle lane	**la piste cyclable**

English word word	French
The path	**l'allée**
The avenue	**l'avenue**
The ditch	**le fossé**
The pedestrian crossing	**le passage piéton**
The light	**le feu**
The road sign	**le panneau de signalisation**
The park	**le parc**

English word word	French
The city centre	**le centre-ville**
The suburb	**la banlieue**
The industrial area	**la zone industrielle**

The field   le terrain

The flat   l'appartement

The block   le pâté de maison

The building   l'immeuble

The district   le quartier

The shop   le magasin

English word   French word

Commercial premises le local commercial

The house   la maison

The shopping mall   le centre commercial

Dialogs

<u>Dialog 1</u>

I need to go to the city today.   **Je dois aller en ville aujourd'hui.**

Sure, you can use my car.   **Bien sûr, tu peux utiliser ma voiture.**

<u>Dialog 2</u>

John is a very shy boy.   **John est un garçon très timide.**

He comes from the countryside, he is new.   **Il vient de la campagne, il est nouveau.**

<u>Dialog 3</u>

Where is the post office?   **Où est la poste?**

It is in the street behind you.   **Elle est dans la
rue derrière toi.**

<u>Dialog 4</u>

Where is your school located?   **Où   ton
école est-elle située ?**

It is located in the city centre.   **Elle   est
dans le centre-ville.**

Practice

English :   city

French :   **ville**

Repeat :   **ville**

Repeat :   **ville**

Spell :   **v-i-l-l-e**

Spell :   **v-i-l-l-e**

In a phrase :   **Je dois aller en ville aujourd'hui.**   *I need to go
to the city today.*

Repeat :   **Je dois aller en ville aujourd'hui.**   *I need to go
to the city today.*

Repeat :   **Je dois aller en ville aujourd'hui.**   *I need to go to the city today.*

Repeat :   **Je dois aller en ville aujourd'hui.**   *I need to go to the city today.*

English :   countryside

French :   **campagne**

Repeat :   **campagne**

Repeat :   **campagne**

Spell :   **c-a-m-p-a-g-n-e**

Spell :   **c-a-m-p-a-g-n-e**

In a phrase : **Il vient de la campagne, il est nouveau.**   *He comes from the countryside, he is new.*

Repeat :   **Il vient de la campagne, il est nouveau.**   *He comes from the countryside, he is new.*

Repeat :   **Il vient de la campagne, il est nouveau.**   *He comes from the countryside, he is new.*

Repeat :   **Il vient de la campagne, il est nouveau.**   *He comes from the countryside, he is new.*

English :   street

French :   **rue**

Repeat :   **rue**

Repeat :   **rue**

Spell :   **r-u-e**

Spell :   **r-u-e**

In a phrase : **Elle est dans la rue derrière toi. .. *It is in the street behind you.***

Repeat :   **Elle est dans la rue derrière toi. .. *It is in the street behind you.***

Repeat :   **Elle est dans la rue derrière toi. .. *It is in the street behind you.***

Repeat :   **Elle est dans la rue derrière toi. .. *It is in the street behind you.***

English :   city centre

French :   **centre-ville**

Repeat :   **centre-ville**

Repeat :   **centre-ville**

Spell :   **c-e-n-t-r-e-v-i-l-l-e**

Spell :   **c-e-n-t-r-e-v-i-l-l-e**

In a phrase : **Elle est dans le centre-ville.** *It is in the city-centre.*

Repeat : **Elle est dans le centre-ville.** *It is in the city-centre.*

Repeat : **Elle est dans le centre-ville.** *It is in the city-centre.*

Repeat : **Elle est dans le centre-ville.** *It is in the city-centre.*

PLACES & SHOPS

Vocabulary

English word	French word
The shopping mall	**le centre commercial**
The clothes shop	**le magasin de vêtements**
The shoe shop	**le magasin de chaussures**
The cinema	**le cinéma**
The theater	**le théâtre**
The post office	**la poste**
The sports centre	**le centre sportif**
The café	**le café**
The bank	**la banque**
The factory	**l'usine**

The library	la bibliothèque
The school	l'école
The bus stop	l'arrêt de bus
The train station	la gare ferroviaire
The castle	le château
The airport	l'aéroport
The fire station	la caserne de pompiers

English word	French word
The telephone booth	la cabine téléphonique
The hospital	l'hôpital
The garage	le garage

The police station	le poste de police
The church	l'église
The restaurant	le restaurant
The museum	le musée
The zoo	le zoo
The butcher's	le boucher
The car park	le parking
The supermarket	le supermarché
The swimming-pool	la piscine
The dental office	le cabinet dentaire
The medical office	le cabinet médical
The greengrocer	le marchand de fruits et légumes

The petrol station   **la station essence**

The bakery   **la boulangerie**

The fast-food restaurant **le fast-food**

Dialogs

Dialog 1

I would like to buy new shoes. **J'aimerais acheter de nouvelles chaussures.**

There is a new shoe shop in town. **Il y a un nouveau magasin de chaussures en ville.**

Dialog 2

Can we go to the library? **Pouvons-nous aller à la bibliothèque ?**

Sure, we'll go there later. **Bien-sûr, nous irons là-bas plus tard.**

Dialog 3

When do you go back to school? **Quand retournes-tu à l'école ?**

I'll go back there next Monday. **J'y retournerai lundi prochain.**

Dialog 4

We need to buy some milk. **Nous devons acheter du lait.**

Let's go to the supermarket! **Allons au supermarché !**

Practice

English :   shop

French :   **magasin**

Repeat :   **magasin**

Repeat :   **magasin**

Spell :   **m-a-g-a-s-i-n**

Spell :   **m-a-g-a-s-i-n**

In a phrase : **Il y a un nouveau magasin de chaussures en ville.** *There is a new shoe shop in town.*

Repeat :   **Il y a un nouveau magasin de chaussures en ville.** *There is a new shoe shop in town.*

Repeat :   **Il y a un nouveau magasin de chaussures en ville.** *There is a new shoe shop in town.*

Repeat :   **Il y a un nouveau magasin de chaussures en ville.** *There is a new shoe shop in town.*

English :   library

French :   **bibliothèque**

Repeat :   **bibliothèque**

Repeat :   **bibliothèque**

Spell :   **b-i-b-l-i-o-t-h-è-q-u-e**

Spell :   **b-i-b-l-i-o-t-h-è-q-u-e**

In a phrase : **Pouvons-nous aller à la bibliothèque ?** *Can we go to the library?*

Repeat :   **Pouvons-nous aller à la bibliothèque ?** *Can we go to the library?*

Repeat :   **Pouvons-nous aller à la bibliothèque ?** *Can we go to the library?*

Repeat :   **Pouvons-nous aller à la bibliothèque ?** *Can we go to the library?*

English :   school

French :   **école**

Repeat :   **école**

Repeat :   **école**

Spell :   **é-c-o-l-e**

Spell :   **é-c-o-l-e**

In a phrase : **Quand retournes-tu à l'école ?** *When do you go back to school?*

Repeat : **Quand retournes-tu à l'école ?** *When do you go back to school?*

Repeat : **Quand retournes-tu à l'école ?** *When do you go back to school?*

Repeat : **Quand retournes-tu à l'école ?** *When do you go back to school?*

English : supermarket

French : **supermarché**

Repeat : **supermarché**

Repeat : **supermarché**

Spell : **s-u-p-e-r-m-a-r-c-h-é**

Spell : **s-u-p-e-r-m-a-r-c-h-é**

In a phrase : **Allons au supermarché !** *Let's go to the supermarket!*

Repeat : **Allons au supermarché !** *Let's go to the supermarket!*

Repeat : **Allons au supermarché !** *Let's go to the supermarket!*

Repeat : **Allons au supermarché !** *Let's go to the supermarket!*

Chapter 9: GEOGRAPHY

Here is a list of useful names you'll need to know in French if you go on holidays or if you talk about geography in French.

CITIES

Vocabulary

<u>English word</u> word

<u>French</u>

Paris **Paris**

Marseille **Marseille**

Lyon **Lyon**

Toulouse **Toulouse**

Nice **Nice**

Nantes **Nantes**

Strasburg **Strasbourg**

Montpellier **Montpellier**

Toronto **Toronto**

Montreal **Montréal**

Ottawa **Ottawa**

Winnipeg **Winnipeg**

Vancouver **Vancouver**

Dublin **Dublin**

Cork **Cork**

Limerick **Limerick**

Galway
Galway

Waterford
Waterford

New York **New-York**

Los Angeles **Los Angeles**

English word word	French

Chigaco
Chicago

Houston
Houston

Phoenix
Phoenix

Philadelphia
Philadelphie

San Francisco **San Fransisco**

Denver **Denver**

Boston **Boston**

London
Londres

Birmingham
Birmingham

Leeds **Leeds**

Glasgow
Glasgow

Manchester
Manchester

Edinburgh
Edimbourg

Cardiff **Cardiff**

Belfast **Belfast**

Sydney **Sydney**

Melbourne
Melbourne

Brisbane
Brisbane

Perth **Perth**

Adelaide
Adélaide

Canberra
Canberra

Dialogs

<u>Dialog 1</u>

Where does he live? **Où vit-il?**

He lives in London. **Il vit à Londres.**

<u>Dialog 2</u>

Where were you last summer? **Où étais-tu l'été dernier ?**

I was in Edinburgh. **J'étais à Edimbourg.**

<u>Dialog 3</u>

Where do you come from? **D'où viens-tu ?**

I come from Philadelphia. **Je viens de Philadelphie.**

<u>Dialog 4</u>

Which city is gorgeous in France? **Quelle ville est superbe en France ?**

I like Strasburg. **J'aime bien Strasbourg.**

Practice

English :   London

French :   **Londres**

Repeat :   **Londres**

Repeat :   **Londres**

Spell :   **L-o-n-d-r-e-s**

Spell :   **L-o-n-d-r-e-s**

In a phrase :   **Il vit à Londres.** *He lives in London.*

Repeat :   **Il vit à Londres.** *He lives in London.*

Repeat :   **Il vit à Londres.** *He lives in London.*

Repeat :   **Il vit à Londres.** *He lives in London.*

English :   Edinburgh

French :   **Edimbourg**

Repeat :   **Edimbourg**

Repeat :   **Edimbourg**

Spell :   **E-d-i-m-b-o-u-r-g**

Spell :   **E-d-i-m-b-o-u-r-g**

In a phrase : **J'étais à Edimbourg.** *I was in Edinburgh.*

Repeat : **J'étais à Edimbourg.** *I was in Edinburgh.*

Repeat : **J'étais à Edimbourg.** *I was in Edinburgh.*

Repeat : **J'étais à Edimbourg.** *I was in Edinburgh.*

English : Philadelphia

French : **Philadelphie**

Repeat : **Philadelphie**

Repeat : **Philadelphie**

Spell : **P-h-i-l-a-d-e-l-p-h-i-e**

Spell : **P-h-i-l-a-d-e-l-p-h-i-e**

In a phrase : **Je viens de Philadelphie.** *I come from Philadelphia.*

Repeat : **Je viens de Philadelphie.** *I come from Philadelphia.*

Repeat : **Je viens de Philadelphie.** *I come from Philadelphia.*

Repeat : **Je viens de Philadelphie.** *I come from Philadelphia.*

English :   Strasburg

French :   **Strasbourg**

Repeat :   **Strasbourg**

Repeat :   **Strasbourg**

Spell :   **S-t-r-a-s-b-o-u-r-g**

Spell :   **S-t-r-a-s-b-o-u-r-g**

In a phrase :   **J'aime bien Strasbourg.**   *I like Strasburg.*

Repeat :   **J'aime bien Strasbourg.**   *I like Strasburg.*

Repeat :   **J'aime bien Strasbourg.**   *I like Strasburg.*

Repeat :   **J'aime bien Strasbourg.**   *I like Strasburg.*

COUNTRIES

Vocabulary

<u>English word</u>

    <u>French word</u>

The continent

    le continent

America

    l'Amérique

Oceania

    l'Océanie

Asia

    l'Asie

Africa

    l'Afrique

Europe
l'Europe

The country
le pays

Algeria
Algérie

Argentina
Argentine

Australia
Australie

Austria
Autriche

Belgium
Belgique

Brazil
Brésil

Canada
Canada

China
Chine

Colombia
Colombie

Denmark
Danemark

Egypt
Egypte

Estonia
Estonie

Finland
Finlande

France
France

Georgia
Géorgie

Germany
Allemagne

Greece
Grèce

Hungary
Hongrie

Iceland
Islande

India
Inde

Indonesia
Indonésie

<u>English word</u>   <u>French word</u>

Iran	**Iran**	Portugal	
Iraq	**Iraq**		**Portugal**
Ireland		Romania	
	Irlande		**Roumanie**
Israel	**Israel**	Russia	**Russie**
Italy	**Italie**	Serbia	**Serbie**
Jamaïca		South Africa	**Afrique du Sud**
	Jamaïque	South Korea	**Corée du Sud**
Japan	**Japon**	Spain	**Espagne**
Mexico		Sweden	**Suède**
	Mexique	Switzerland	**Suisse**
Morocco	**Maroc**	Syria	**Syrie**
The Netherlands	**les Pays Bas**	Tunisia	**Tunisie**
New-Zealand	**Nouvelle Zélande**	Turkey	**Turquie**
North-Korea	**Corée du Nord**	The United Kingdom	**le Royaume-Uni**
Norway	**Norvège**	The United States of America	**les Etats-Unis**
Poland	**Pologne**		

Dialogs

Dialog 1

What do you know about France? **Que savez-vous de le France ?**

I've heard about Paris. **J'ai entendu parler de Paris.**

Dialog 2

Where do you come from? **D'où viens-tu ?**

I come from the United States. **Je viens des Etats-Unis.**

Dialog 3

Where is London located? **Où se trouve Londres ?**

London is in the United Kingdom. **Londres est au Royaume-Uni.**

Dialog 4

Which country was the source of the WWII? **Quel pays était la source de la Seconde Guerre Mondiale ?**

Germany was the source. **L'Allemagne en était la source.**

Practice

English :   France

French :   **France**

Repeat :   **France**

Repeat :   **France**

Spell :   **F-r-a-n-c-e**

Spell :   **F-r-a-n-c-e**

In a phrase : **Que savez-vous de le France ?** *What do you know about France?*

Repeat :   **Que savez-vous de le France ?** *What do you know about France?*

Repeat :   **Que savez-vous de le France ?** *What do you know about France?*

Repeat :   **Que savez-vous de le France ?** *What do you know about France?*

English :   The United States of America

French :   **Les Etats-Unis**

Repeat :   **Les Etats-Unis**

Repeat :   **Les Etats-Unis**

Spell :   **E-t-a-t-s-U-n-i-s**

Spell :   **E-t-a-t-s-U-n-i-s**

In a phrase : **Je viens des Etats-Unis.** *I come from the United States of America.*

Repeat :   **Je viens des Etats-Unis.** *I come from the United States of America.*

Repeat :   **Je viens des Etats-Unis.** *I come from the United States of America.*

Repeat :   **Je viens des Etats-Unis.** *I come from the United States of America.*

English :   The United-Kingdom

French :   **Le Royaume-Uni**

Repeat :   **Le Royaume-Uni**

Repeat :   **Le Royaume-Uni**

Spell :   **R-o-y-a-u-m-e-U-n-i**

Spell :   **R-o-y-a-u-m-e-U-n-i**

In a phrase : **Londres est au Royaume-Uni.** *London is in the United Kingdom.*

Repeat :   **Londres est au Royaume-Uni.** *London is in the United Kingdom.*

Repeat :   **Londres est au Royaume-Uni.** *London is in the United Kingdom.*

Repeat :   **Londres est au Royaume-Uni.** *London is in the United Kingdom.*

English :   Germany

French :   **Allemagne**

Repeat :   **Allemagne**

Repeat :   **Allemagne**

Spell :   **A-l-l-e-m-a-g-n-e**

Spell :   **A-l-l-e-m-a-g-n-e**

In a phrase : **L'Allemagne en était la source.** *Germany was the source.*

Repeat :   **L'Allemagne en était la source.** *Germany was the source.*

Repeat :   **L'Allemagne en était la source.** *Germany was the source.*

Repeat :   **L'Allemagne en était la source.** *Germany was the source.*

Vocabulary

English word word	French	English word word	French
The landscape	**le paysage**	The cliff	**la falaise**
The river	**la rivière, le fleuve**	The isle	**l'île**
The valley	**la vallée**	The beach	**la plage**
The mountain	**la montagne**	The shore	**le rivage**
The field	**le champ**	The rock	**le rocher**
The plain	**la plaine**	The tide	**la marée**
The bay	**la baie**	The swamp	**le marécage**

Dialogs

Dialog 1

Which cliffs do you know in France? **Quelles falaises connais-tu en France ?**

Etretat in Normandy. **Etretat en Normandie.**

Dialog 2

What is the name of the river in Paris? **Quel est le nom du fleuve à Paris ?**

La Seine. **La Seine.**

Dialog 3

Which landscape do you like the most? **Quel paysage connais-tu le mieux ?**

I love mountains. **J'adore les montagnes.**

Dialog 4

You'll see amazing landscapes in Brittany. **Tu verras des paysages incroyables en Bretagne.**

There are beautiful beaches there. **Il y a des belles plages là-bas.**

Practice

English :   cliff

French :   **falaise**

Repeat :   **falaise**

Repeat :   **falaise**

Spell :   **f-a-l-a-i-s-e**

Spell :   **f-a-l-a-i-s-e**

In a phrase :   **Quelles falaises connais-tu en France ?**   *Which cliffs do you know in France?*

Repeat :   **Quelles falaises connais-tu en France ?**   *Which cliffs do you know in France?*

Repeat :   **Quelles falaises connais-tu en France ?**   *Which cliffs do you know in France?*

Repeat :   **Quelles falaises connais-tu en France ?**   *Which cliffs do you know in France?*

English :   river

French :   **fleuve**

Repeat :   **fleuve**

Repeat :   **fleuve**

Spell :   **f-l-e-u-v-e**

Spell :   **f-l-e-u-v-e**

In a phrase :   **Quel est le nom du fleuve à Paris ?** *What is the name of the river in Paris?*

Repeat :   **Quel est le nom du fleuve à Paris ?** *What is the name of the river in Paris?*

Repeat :   **Quel est le nom du fleuve à Paris ?** *What is the name of the river in Paris?*

Repeat :   **Quel est le nom du fleuve à Paris ?** *What is the name of the river in Paris?*

English :   mountain

French :   **montagne**

Repeat :   **montagne**

Repeat :   **montagne**

Spell :   **m-o-n-t-a-g-n-e**

Spell :   **m-o-n-t-a-g-n-e**

In a phrase :   **J'adore les montagnes.** *I love mountains.*

Repeat :   **J'adore les montagnes.** *I love mountains.*

Repeat :   **J'adore les montagnes.** *I love mountains.*

Repeat :   **J'adore les montagnes.** *I love mountains.*

English :   beach

French :   **plage**

Repeat :   **plage**

Repeat :   **plage**

Spell :   **p-l-a-g-e**

Spell :   **p-l-a-g-e**

In a phrase : **Il y a des belles plages là-bas.**   *There are beautiful beaches there.*

Repeat :   **Il y a des belles plages là-bas.** *There are beautiful beaches there.*

Repeat :   **Il y a des belles plages là-bas.** *There are beautiful beaches there.*

Repeat :   **Il y a des belles plages là-bas.** *There are beautiful beaches there.*

Chapter 10: THE WEATHER

When talking about the everyday life, you'll obviously talk about the weather. Discover how you can say that it is rainy or sunny in French !

THE WEATHER

Vocabulary

English word word	French
Hot	**chaud**
Sunny	**ensoleillé**
Cloudy	**nuageux**
Rainy	**pluvieux**
Foggy	**brumeux**
Snowy	**neigeux**
Windy	**venteux**

	French
Stormy	**orageux**
Cold	**froid**
Cool	**frais**
Dry	**sec**
Rain	**pluie**
Shower	**averse**
Mist	**brouillard**

English word word	French
Fog	**brume**
Drizzle	**bruine**

Flood
inondation

Snow **neige**

Freezing **glacé**

Gloomy
sombre

Overcast **couvert**

Breeze **brise**

Gale
tempête

Hurricane
ouragan

Drought
secheresse

Lightning **éclair**

Thunder
tonnerre

Rainbow **arc-en-ciel**

Dialogs

<u>Dialog 1</u>

What's the weather like today? **Quel temps fait-il aujourd'hui ?**

It is rainy and cloudy. **C'est pluvieux et nuageux.**

<u>Dialog 2</u>

Let's watch the weather forecast. **Regardons les prévisions météo.**

It's going to be sunny in the region. **Le temps sera ensoleillé dans la région.**

<u>Dialog 3</u>

Have you heard the forecast? **As-tu entendu les prévisions ?**

Yes, there will be showers today. **Oui, il y aura des averses aujourd'hui.**

<u>Dialog 4</u>

It's so hot today. **Il fait si chaud aujourd'hui.**

It is not surprising during the summer. **Ce n'est pas surprenant pendant l'été.**

Practice

English :   rainy

French :   **pluvieux**

Repeat :   **pluvieux**

Repeat :   **pluvieux**

Spell :   **p-l-u-v-i-e-u-x**

Spell :   **p-l-u-v-i-e-u-x**

In a phrase : **C'est pluvieux et nuageux.** *It's rainy and cloudy.*

Repeat :   **C'est pluvieux et nuageux.** *It's rainy and cloudy.*

Repeat :   **C'est pluvieux et nuageux.**   *It's rainy and cloudy.*

Repeat :   **C'est pluvieux et nuageux.**   *It's rainy and cloudy.*

English :   sunny

French :   **ensoleillé**

Repeat :   **ensoleillé**

Repeat :   **ensoleillé**

Spell :   **e-n-s-o-l-e-i-l-l-é**

Spell :   **e-n-s-o-l-e-i-l-l-é**

In a phrase :   **Le temps sera ensoleillé dans la région.**   *It's going to be sunny in the region.*

Repeat :   **Le temps sera ensoleillé dans la région.**   *It's going to be sunny in the region.*

Repeat :   **Le temps sera ensoleillé dans la région.**   *It's going to be sunny in the region.*

Repeat :   **Le temps sera ensoleillé dans la région.**   *It's going to be sunny in the region.*

English :   hot

French :   **chaud**

Repeat :   **chaud**

Repeat :   **chaud**

Spell :   **c-h-a-u-d**

Spell :   **c-h-a-u-d**

In a phrase :   **Il fait si chaud aujourd'hui.**   *It is so hot today.*

Repeat :   **Il fait si chaud aujourd'hui.**   *It is so hot today.*

Repeat :   **Il fait si chaud aujourd'hui.**   *It is so hot today.*

Repeat :   **Il fait si chaud aujourd'hui.**   *It is so hot today.*

Chapter 11: COMMUNICATION

We are surrounded by information every single day. It is important to know how to talk about the news in French as well if you want to speak French.

THE NEWS

Vocabulary

English word word	French		
A newspaper	**un journal**	The television	**la television**
A magazine	**un magazine**	The news	**les informations**
A piece of information	**une information**	To follow the news	**suivre les infos**
A show	**une émission**	To break the news	**annoncer les infos**
A newsletter	**un bulletin**	An announcement	**une annonce**
The radio	**la radio**	The small ads	**les petites announces**
		An advert	**une publicité**

English word word	French
A column	**une rubrique**
National news	**les infos nationales**
Local news	**les infos régionales**
Classifies ads	**les annonces classées**
The headline	**le gros titre**
To break into	**faire la une**
The weather forecast	**les prévisions météo**
Advice	**des conseils**
A cartoon	**un dessin**
Entertainement	**le divertissement**
A gossip	**un ragot**
A comic	**une bande-dessinée**
The love column	**le courrier du coeur**
Death notice	**avis de décès**
An alert	**une alerte**

Dialogs

Dialog 1

Do you want to watch TV? **Veux-tu regarder la télévision ?**

Yes, there is a famous TV show. **Oui, il y a une émission télé connue.**

Dialog 2

Don't forget to buy the local newspaper. **N'oublie pas
d'acheter le journal du coin.**

Sure. **Bien sûr.**

Dialog 3

Kellogg's is still the best for breakfast. **Kellog's
est toujours la meilleure pour le petit-déjeuner.**

Yes, its advert is famous. **Oui, sa publicité
est connue.**

Dialog 4

Have you read the headlines in the newspaper? **As-tu lu les gros
titres du journal ?**

No, what happened? **Non, que s'est-il
passé ?**

English : show

French : **émission**

Repeat : **émission**

Repeat : **émission**

Spell : **é-m-i-s-s-i-o-n**

Spell : **é-m-i-s-s-i-o-n**

In a phrase :   **Oui, il y a une émission télé connue.**   *There is a famous TV show.*

Repeat :   **Oui, il y a une émission télé connue.**   *There is a famous TV show.*

Repeat :   **Oui, il y a une émission télé connue.**   *There is a famous TV show.*

Repeat :   **Oui, il y a une émission télé connue.**   *There is a famous TV show.*

English :   newspaper

French :   **journal**

Repeat :   **journal**

Repeat :   **journal**

Spell :   **j-o-u-r-n-a-l**

Spell :   **j-o-u-r-n-a-l**

In a phrase :   **N'oublie pas d'acheter le journal du coin.**   *Don't forget to buy the local newspaper.*

Repeat :   **N'oublie pas d'acheter le journal du coin.**
Don't forget to buy the local newspaper.

Repeat :   **N'oublie pas d'acheter le journal du coin.**
Don't forget to buy the local newspaper.

Repeat :   **N'oublie pas d'acheter le journal du coin.**
Don't forget to buy the local newspaper.

English :   advert

French :   **publicité**

Repeat :   **publicité**

Repeat :   **publicité**

Spell :   **p-u-b-l-i-c-i-t-é**

Spell :   **p-u-b-l-i-c-i-t-é**

In a phrase :   **Oui, sa publicité est connue.**   ***Yes, its advert is famous.***

Repeat :   **Oui, sa publicité est connue.**   ***Yes, its advert is famous.***

Repeat :   **Oui, sa publicité est connue.**   ***Yes, its advert is famous.***

Repeat :   **Oui, sa publicité est connue.**   ***Yes, its advert is famous.***

English :   headline

French :   **gros titre**

Repeat :   **gros titre**

Repeat :   **gros titre**

Spell :   **g-r-o-s-t-i-t-r-e**

Spell :   **g-r-o-s-t-i-t-r-e**

In a phrase :   **As-tu lu les gros titres du journal ?** *Have you read the headlines in the newspaper?*

Repeat :   **As-tu lu les gros titres du journal ?** *Have you read the headlines in the newspaper?*

Repeat :   **As-tu lu les gros titres du journal ?** *Have you read the headlines in the newspaper?*

Repeat :   **As-tu lu les gros titres du journal ?** *Have you read the headlines in the newspaper?*

INTERNET

Vocabulary

English word word	French	A page	**une page**
A connection	**une connexion**	To sign up	**s'inscrire**
A browser	**un navigateur**	English word word	French

The subscription **l'abonnement**	An app **une application**
To log in **Se connecter**	A research **une recherche**
An online newspaper **un journal en ligne**	A key-word **un mot clé**
A magazine **un magazine**	Instant messenger **messagerie instantanée**
A forum **un forum**	A computer **un ordinateur**
A blog **un blog**	A laptop **un PC portable**
A social network **un réseau social**	

Dialogs

<u>Dialog 1</u>

There is no internet connection. **Il n'y a pas de connexion internet.**

Check your browser. **Vérifie ton navigateur.**

<u>Dialog 2</u>

How can I use Facebook? **Comment puis-je utiliser Facebook ?**

You need to log into your account.
connecter à ton compte.

Tu   dois   te

Dialog 3

I have to do some research online.
recherches en ligne.

Je dois faire des

Use key words.
mots clés.

Utilise les

Dialog 4

Do you have a computer?
ordinateur ?

As-tu   un

Yes, it is in the bedroom.
la chambre.

Oui, il est dans

Practice

English :   browser

French :   **navigateur**

Repeat :   **navigateur**

Repeat :   **navigateur**

Spell :   **n-a-v-i-g-a-t-e-u-r**

Spell :   **n-a-v-i-g-a-t-e-u-r**

In a phrase :   **Vérifie ton navigateur.** *Check your browser.*

Repeat :   **Vérifie ton navigateur.** *Check your browser.*

Repeat :   **Vérifie ton navigateur.** *Check your browser.*

Repeat :   **Vérifie ton navigateur.** *Check your browser.*

English :   log in

French :   **se connecter**

Repeat :   **se connecter**

Repeat :   **se connecter**

Spell :   **s-e-c-o-n-n-e-c-t-e-r**

Spell :   **s-e-c-o-n-n-e-c-t-e-r**

In a phrase :   **Tu dois te connecter à ton compte.** *You need to log into your account.*

Repeat :   **Tu dois te connecter à ton compte.** *You need to log into your account.*

Repeat :   **Tu dois te connecter à ton compte.** *You need to log into your account.*

Repeat :   **Tu dois te connecter à ton compte.** *You need to log into your account.*

English :   research

French :   **recherche**

Repeat :   **recherche**

Repeat :   **recherche**

Spell :   **r-e-c-h-e-r-c-h-e**

Spell :   **r-e-c-h-e-r-c-h-e**

In a phrase : **Je dois faire des recherches en ligne.** *I have to do some research online.*

Repeat :   **Je dois faire des recherches en ligne.** *I have to do some research online.*

Repeat :   **Je dois faire des recherches en ligne.** *I have to do some research online.*

Repeat :   **Je dois faire des recherches en ligne.** *I have to do some research online.*

English :   computer

French :   **ordinateur**

Repeat :   **ordinateur**

Repeat :   **ordinateur**

Spell :   **o-r-d-i-n-a-t-e-u-r**

Spell :   **o-r-d-i-n-a-t-e-u-r**

In a phrase : **As-tu un ordinateur ?** *Do you have a computer?*

Repeat : **As-tu un ordinateur ?** *Do you have a computer?*

Repeat : **As-tu un ordinateur ?** *Do you have a computer?*

Repeat : **As-tu un ordinateur ?** *Do you have a computer?*

SOCIAL NETWORKS

Vocabulary

English word word	French		
A social network	**un réseau social**	To log into	**se connecter**
A connection	**une connexion**	To sign up	**s'inscrire**
Online	**en ligne**	A page	**une page**
An account	**un compte**	Instant messenger	**Messagerie instantanée**
A profile	**un profil**	To post	**poster**

English word	French word
To publish	**publier**
A message	**un message**
A friend	**un ami**
A link	**un lien**
An acquaintance	**une connaissance**
To follow a page	**suivre une page**
The news	**l'actualité**
An advert	**une publicité**
A photo	**une photo**
A video	**une vidéo**

Dialogs

<u>Dialog 1</u>

You are addicted to social networks. **Tu es accro aux réseaux sociaux.**

No, I just use them twice a day. **Non, je ne l'utilise que deux fois par jour.**

<u>Dialog 2</u>

Do you follow the news? **Suis-tu l'actualité ?**

Yes, I read online newspapers. **Oui, je lis la presse en ligne.**

<u>Dialog 3</u>

How many friends do you have on Facebook? **Combien d'amis as-tu sur Facebook ?**

I have more than 200 friends. **J'ai plus de 200 amis.**

Dialog 4

There are too many adverts on Facebook. **Il y a trop de publicités sur Facebook.**

You can ignore them. **Tu peux les ignorer.**

Practice

English :   social network

French :   **réseau social**

Repeat :   **réseau social**

Repeat :   **réseau social**

Spell :   **r-é-s-e-a-u-s-o-c-i-a-l**

Spell :   **r-é-s-e-a-u-s-o-c-i-a-l**

In a phrase :   **Tu es accro aux réseaux sociaux.**   *You are addicted to social networks.*

Repeat :   **Tu es accro aux réseaux sociaux.**   *You are addicted to social networks.*

Repeat :   **Tu es accro aux réseaux sociaux.**   *You are addicted to social networks.*

Repeat :   **Tu es accro aux réseaux sociaux.**   *You are addicted to social networks.*

English :   online

French :   **en ligne**

Repeat :   **en ligne**

Repeat :   **en ligne**

Spell :   **e-n-l-i-g-n-e**

Spell :   **e-n-l-i-g-n-e**

In a phrase :   **Oui, je lis la presse en ligne.**   *Yes, I read online newspapers.*

Repeat :   **Oui, je lis la presse en ligne.**   *Yes, I read online newspapers.*

Repeat :   **Oui, je lis la presse en ligne.**   *Yes, I read online newspapers.*

Repeat :   **Oui, je lis la presse en ligne.**   *Yes, I read online newspapers.*

English :   friend

French :   **ami**

Repeat :   **ami**

Repeat :   **ami**

Spell :   **a-m-i**

Spell :   **a-m-i**

In a phrase : **Combien d'amis as-tu sur Facebook ?**   *How many friends do you have on Facebook?*

Repeat :   **Combien d'amis as-tu sur Facebook ?**   *How many friends do you have on Facebook?*

Repeat :   **Combien d'amis as-tu sur Facebook ?**   *How many friends do you have on Facebook?*

Repeat :   **Combien d'amis as-tu sur Facebook ?**   *How many friends do you have on Facebook?*

English :   advert

French :   **publicité**

Repeat :   **publicité**

Repeat :   **publicité**

Spell :   **p-u-b-l-i-c-i-t-é**

Spell :   **p-u-b-l-i-c-i-t-é**

In a phrase :   **Il y a trop de publicités sur Facebook.** *There are too many adverts on Facebook.*

Repeat :   **Il y a trop de publicités sur Facebook.** *There are too many adverts on Facebook.*

Repeat :   **Il y a trop de publicités sur Facebook.** *There are too many adverts on Facebook.*

Repeat :   **Il y a trop de publicités sur Facebook.** *There are too many adverts on Facebook.*

ON THE PHONE

Vocabulary

English word word	French
A phone	**un téléphone**
A mobile phone	**un téléphone**
A cell phone	**un téléphone**
A flip phone	**un téléphone à clapet**

A tablet computer	**une tablette tactile**
The screen	**l'écran**
The key	**la touche**
The ring	**la sonnerie**

English word word	French
The alert	**l'alerte**

A call **un appel**

To make a phone call **passer un appel**

To receive **recevoir**

To answer **répondre**

Dialogs

Dialog 1

I need to call my mother. **Je dois appeler ma mère.**

Use my mobile phone. **Utilise mon téléphone portable.**

Dialog 2

Your phone is ringing. **Ton téléphone sonne.**

Yes, it must be my mother. **Oui, ce doit être ma mère.**

Dialog 3

I need to make a phone call. **Je dois passer un coup de fil.**

To leave a message **laisser un message**

The answering machine **Le répondeur**

To send a message **envoyer un message**

Use my mobile phone. **Utilise mon téléphone portable.**

<u>Dialog 4</u>

Your phone is ringing. **Ton téléphone sonne.**

I don't want to answer. **Je ne veux pas répondre.**

Practice

English :   mobile phone

French :   **téléphone portable**

Repeat :   **téléphone portable**

Repeat :   **téléphone portable**

Spell :   **t-é-l-é-p-h-o-n-e-p-o-r-t-a-b-l-e**

Spell :   **t-é-l-é-p-h-o-n-e-p-o-r-t-a-b-l-e**

In a phrase : **Utilise mon téléphone portable.** *Use my mobile phone.*

Repeat : **Utilise mon téléphone portable.** *Use my mobile phone.*

Repeat : **Utilise mon téléphone portable.** *Use my mobile phone.*

Repeat :   **Utilise mon téléphone portable.** *Use my mobile phone.*

English :   ring

French :   **sonner**

Repeat :   **sonner**

Repeat :   **sonner**

Spell :   **s-o-n-n-e-r**

Spell :   **s-o-n-n-e-r**

In a phrase : **Ton téléphone sonne.** *My phone is ringing.*

Repeat :   **Ton téléphone sonne.** *My phone is ringing.*

Repeat :   **Ton téléphone sonne.** *My phone is ringing.*

Repeat :   **Ton téléphone sonne.** *My phone is ringing.*

English :   call

French :   **appel**

Repeat :   **appel**

Repeat :   **appel**

Spell :   **a-p-p-e-l**

Spell :   **a-p-p-e-l**

In a phrase : **Je dois passer un coup de fil.** *I need to make a phone call.*

Repeat : **Je dois passer un coup de fil.** *I need to make a phone call.*

Repeat : **Je dois passer un coup de fil.** *I need to make a phone call.*

Repeat : **Je dois passer un coup de fil.** *I need to make a phone call.*

English : answer

French : **répondre**

Repeat : **répondre**

Repeat : **répondre**

Spell : **r-é-p-o-n-d-r-e**

Spell : **r-é-p-o-n-d-r-e**

In a phrase : **Je ne veux pas répondre.** *I don't want to answer.*

Repeat : **Je ne veux pas répondre.** *I don't want to answer.*

Repeat : **Je ne veux pas répondre.** *I don't want to answer.*

Repeat : **Je ne veux pas répondre.** *I don't want to answer.*

Chapter 12: CELEBRATIONS

You can also enjoy parties and celebrations in your everyday life.
They are moments where you meet people and you may need to speak
French during these events.

PARTIES & CELEBRATIONS

Vocabulary

English word word	French		
A party	**une fête**	A wedding	**un mariage**
An evening	**une soirée**	A funeral	**des obsèques**
A celebration	**une festivité**	A baptism	**un baptême**
An event	**un événement**	An invitation	**une invitation**
A festival	**un festival**	An answer	**une réponse**
A concert	**un concert**	A card	**une carte**
		An add	**une annonce**

English word	French word		English word	French word
To party, celebrate	**faire la fête**		Make-up	**du maquillage**
To go to	**aller à**		Christmas	**Noël**
Activities	**des activités**		New Year	**Nouvel An**
A decoration	**une décoration**		The eve	**la veille**
A poster	**une affiche**		Candlemas	**la Chandeleur**
A leaflet	**une brochure**		Holidays	**des vacances**
Flakes	**des paillettes**		Easter break	**vacances de paques**
A dress, outfit	**un costume**		Summer break	**vacances d'été**
			A bank holiday	**un jour férié**

Dialogs

Dialog 1

Do you want to watch a movie? **Veux-tu voir un film ?**

No, I am invited to a party. **Non, je suis
invitée à une fête.**

Dialog 2

This is an important event. **C'est un
événement important.**

Yes, everybody will be there. **Oui, tout le
monde y sera.**

Dialog 3

I am invited to Sarah's Wedding. **Je suis invitée
au mariage de Sarah.**

She is going to get married! **Elle va se
marier !**

Dialog 4

Where do you stay for Christmas? **Où restes-tu
pour Noël ?**

I'll be at my mother's house. **Je serai chez
ma mère.**

Practice

English :   party

French :   **fête**

Repeat :   **fête**

Repeat :   **fête**

Spell :   **f-ê-t-e**

Spell :   **f-ê-t-e**

In a phrase : **Non, je suis invitée à une fête.** *No, I am invited to a party.*

Repeat :   **Non, je suis invitée à une fête.** *No, I am invited to a party.*

Repeat :   **Non, je suis invitée à une fête.** *No, I am invited to a party.*

Repeat :   **Non, je suis invitée à une fête.** *No, I am invited to a party.*

English :   event

French :   **événement**

Repeat :   **événement**

Repeat :   **événement**

Spell :   **é-v-é-n-e-m-e-n-t**

Spell :   **é-v-é-n-e-m-e-n-t**

In a phrase :   **C'est un événement important.**   *It is an important event.*

Repeat :   **C'est un événement important.**   *It is an important event.*

Repeat :   **C'est un événement important.**   *It is an important event.*

Repeat :   **C'est un événement important.**   *It is an important event.*

English :   wedding

French :   **mariage**

Repeat :   **mariage**

Repeat :   **mariage**

Spell :   **m-a-r-i-a-g-e**

Spell :   **m-a-r-i-a-g-e**

In a phrase :   **Je suis invitée au mariage de Sarah.**   *I am invited to Sarah's wedding.*

Repeat :   **Je suis invitée au mariage de Sarah.**   *I am invited to Sarah's wedding.*

Repeat :   **Je suis invitée au mariage de Sarah.**   *I am invited to Sarah's wedding.*

Repeat :   **Je suis invitée au mariage de Sarah.** *I am invited to Sarah's wedding.*

English :   Christmas

French :   **Noël**

Repeat :   **Noël**

Repeat :   **Noël**

Spell :   **N-o-ë-l**

Spell :   **N-o-ë-l**

In a phrase : **Où restes-tu pour Noël ?** *Where do you stay for Christmas?*

Repeat :   **Où restes-tu pour Noël ?** *Where do you stay for Christmas?*

Repeat :   **Où restes-tu pour Noël ?** *Where do you stay for Christmas?*

Repeat :   **Où restes-tu pour Noël ?** *Where do you stay for Christmas?*

Chapter 13: ON HOLIDAYS

One of the moments you speak a foreign language is when you are on holidays, if you go abroad or if your meet foreigners. Let's review the lexical fields you may need to know in French.

GOING ON HOLIDAYS

Vocabulary

English word word	French		
A car	**une voiture**	A holiday resort	**un village vacances**
A van	**un van**	A tourist site	**un site touristique**
A mobil-home	**un mobile-home**	A tourist attraction	**une attraction touristique**
A camp site	**un camping**	A museum	**un musée**
A hostel	**un hôtel**	The beach	**la plage**
A guest house	**une maison d'hôtes**	The mountains	**les montagnes**
		The train	**le train**

English	French
The boat	le **bateau**
The plane	**l'avion**
A train station	**une gare ferroviaire**
A train ticket	**un billet de train**
On time	**à l'heure**

English word word	French
Delayed	**retardé**
To buy	**acheter**
To book	**réserver**
A Train carriage	**un wagon**
One-way	**aller simple**
Return	**aller-retour**

English	French
Speed	**la vitesse**
The airport	**l'aéroport**
The flight	**le vol**
A stop	**une escale**
Boarding	**embarquement**
A seat	**une place, siège**
A flight ticket	**un billet d'avion**
Jetlag	**décalage horaire**
A cruise	**une croisière**
To go	**aller**
To leave	**quitter**
To stay	**rester**
To go back	**revenir**

Dialogs

Dialog 1

When are you on holidays? **Quand es-tu en vacances ?**

In two days. **Dans deux jours.**

Dialog 2

When do you go to the airport? **Quand vas-tu à l'aéroport ?**

This afternoon. **Cet après-midi.**

Dialog 3

Where is the museum? **Où est le musée ?**

In the street there. **Dans la rue là-bas.**

Dialog 4

Have you seen the new offer? **As-tu vu la nouvelle offre ?**

There is a cruise at a cheap price! **Il y a une croisière pas chère !**

Practice

English :   holidays

French :   **vacances**

Repeat :   **vacances**

Repeat :   **vacances**

Spell :   **v-a-c-a-n-c-e-s**

Spell :   **v-a-c-a-n-c-e-s**

In a phrase :   **Quand es-tu en vacances ?** *When are you on holidays?*

Repeat :   **Quand es-tu en vacances ?** *When are you on holidays?*

Repeat :   **Quand es-tu en vacances ?** *When are you on holidays?*

Repeat :   **Quand es-tu en vacances ?** *When are you on holidays?*

English :   airport

French :   **aéroport**

Repeat :   **aéroport**

Repeat :   **aéroport**

Spell :   **a-é-r-o-p-o-r-t**

Spell :   **a-é-r-o-p-o-r-t**

In a phrase :   **Quand vas-tu à l'aéroport ?**   *When do you go to the airport?*

Repeat :   **Quand vas-tu à l'aéroport ?**   *When do you go to the airport?*

Repeat :   **Quand vas-tu à l'aéroport ?**   *When do you go to the airport?*

Repeat :   **Quand vas-tu à l'aéroport ?**   *When do you go to the airport?*

English :   museum

French :   **musée**

Repeat :   **musée**

Repeat :   **musée**

Spell :   **m-u-s-e-u-m**

Spell :   **m-u-s-e-u-m**

In a phrase :   **Où est le musée ?**   *Where is the museum?*

Repeat :   **Où est le musée ?**   *Where is the museum?*

Repeat :   **Où est le musée ?**   *Where is the museum?*

Repeat :   **Où est le musée ?**   *Where is the museum?*

English :   cruise

French :   **croisière**

Repeat :   **croisière**

Repeat :   **croisière**

Spell :   **c-r-u-i-s-e**

Spell :   **c-r-u-i-s-e**

In a phrase :   **Il y a une croisière pas chère !** *There is a cheap cruise!*

Repeat :   **Il y a une croisière pas chère !** *There is a cheap cruise!*

Repeat :   **Il y a une croisière pas chère !** *There is a cheap cruise!*

Repeat :   **Il y a une croisière pas chère !** *There is a cheap cruise!*

Conclusion

In this book, you've learned key words in French to be able to converse in each situation in your everyday life. You may need to use another language at school, at work, if you meet foreigners or if you go on holidays. The French language has specific pronunciations but you can start with words to understand it and be able to make sentences. The themes developed in this book are the cornerstones that will help you be at ease with the language. The basics are useful list of words you use in various ways (colours, numbers, the date in chapter 1). When talking to someone else, you may talk about yourself, your physical appearance, your emotions (chapter 2) or you may talk about people you met (chapter 3). You will also probably explain what you usually do (chapter 4) and talk about the place where you live (your house, chapter 5). If you are a young person, you will talk about your school (chapter 6) and what you eat (chapter 7). Moreover, it is also important to be able to mention where you go in town (chapter 8) and know how to use names of cities and countries (chapter 9), as well as being able to talk about the weather (chapter 10). One main aspect of your everyday life is information and communication (chapter 11), celebrations you will enjoy (chapter 12) as well as the vocabulary linked to holidays (chapter 13).

These chapters have to be read regularly and you need to feel motivated and interested to learn quickly and remember the words. It is advised to find quiet moments, read and repeat the lists alone, then with someone who can help you. Don't try to learn all the words at the same time or in a short period of time. Learning a foreign language takes years of practice, but you can still enjoy learning key words to understand simple dialogs and be able to communicate.

www.ingramcontent.com/pod-product-compliance
Lightning Source LLC
Chambersburg PA
CBHW022141050726
47590CB00002B/534